A Layman's Commentary

Volume 7

Epistles
of
Paul

**Romans, 1 and 2 Corinthians, Galatians, Ephesians,
Philippians, Colossians, 1 and 2 Thessalonians,
1 and 2 Timothy, Titus, Philemon**

John Devine

BALBOA.
PRESS
A DIVISION OF HAY HOUSE

Balboa Press books may be ordered through booksellers or by contacting:

Balboa Press
A Division of Hay House
1663 Liberty Drive
Bloomington, IN 47403
www.balboapress.com.au
1-(877) 407-4847

ISBN: 978-1-4525-1403-1 (sc)
ISBN: 978-1-4525-1404-8 (e)

Because of the dynamic nature of the Internet, any web addresses or
links contained in this book may have changed since publication and
may no longer be valid. The views expressed in this work are solely those
of the author and do not necessarily reflect the views of the publisher,
and the publisher hereby disclaims any responsibility for them.

The author of this book does not dispense medical advice or prescribe the use
of any technique as a form of treatment for physical, emotional, or medical
problems without the advice of a physician, either directly or indirectly. The
intent of the author is only to offer information of a general nature to help you
in your quest for emotional and spiritual well-being. In the event you use any
of the information in this book for yourself, which is your constitutional right,
the author and the publisher assume no responsibility for your actions.

Any people depicted in stock imagery provided by Thinkstock are models,
and such images are being used for illustrative purposes only.
Certain stock imagery © Thinkstock.

Printed in the United States of America

Balboa Press rev. date: 04/24/2014

CONTENTS

The Epistles of Paul

These thirteen letters were written by Paul the apostle to the churches and leaders in Asia Minor and Southern Europe with whom he was associated. Most of these groups he had been instrumental in forming. The letters include words of instruction and encouragement for the believers in living a victorious and effective life.

They reinforce the content of the sermons of Peter and Paul as recorded in the Book of the Acts of the Apostles.

The Epistles were not written as doctrine or systematic theology but as letters to groups of believers to address issues and provide instruction. However they also contribute to a significant understanding of the doctrine of the Christian faith.

Romans

Introduction – Paul was commissioned by Jesus in a vision to be the Apostle to the Gentiles Acts 9:15,16; 16:15-18. His missionary activities had already extended through Asia Minor to Macedonia and Greece over 12 years. He wanted to go to Rome, capital of Italy as well to preach the Gospel to as many as possible. He eventually achieved this desire indirectly in AD 60 through being arrested in Jerusalem and held under house detention for two years after appealing to Caesar as a Roman citizen Acts 28:30.

Author – The apostle Paul wrote this letter from Corinth around AD 57 in preparation for his planned visit to Rome 15:23-25; 16:23. This was during his third mission Journey and his third visit to Corinth Acts 20:2-6.

Period – Written to the believers in Rome. Many had come to faith as a result of the visitors from Rome who were present in Jerusalem at Pentecost Acts 2:8-11. There were a significant number of house churches. Paul wanted to prepare them for his anticipated first visit by sending this great doctrinal letter Acts 19:21.

Theme – Eternal Life through Faith in Christ alone This is the most organized statement of the Christian faith in relation to Judaism, describing the doctrine of salvation by grace through faith in Christ alone.

Having been a zealous Pharisee Paul found great joy at being able to come into a personal relationship with God through Jesus. This freed him from the burden of self-justification through obeying laws and customs. The Book of Romans has had great impact on many including Augustine 386, Martin Luther 1515 and John Wesley 1738. It has changed countless lives since first written and continues to do so throughout the world today.

An overview of the finished work of Jesus, as set out in the Book of Romans -

• God's righteous judgment will come on sinful mankind and they will be without excuse 1:18; 2:16

• The consequence (penalty) of falling short of God's nature is separation from God 6:23

• Mankind is unable to keep the requirements of the law for all have sinned - we come short of God's nature 3:19,20,23

- God's gift of righteousness through faith in Christ alone is available to all who believe in him 1:17; 3:21-24. God presented Jesus as a sacrifice of atonement through faith in his blood removing the offense of our sin before God 3:25
- Being justified by faith in our Lord Jesus Christ we have peace with God and access to God's presence 5:1,8
- We have been freed from sin to live holy lives and gain eternal life 6:22,23
- We have new life and a whole new outlook because God's Holy Spirit now lives in the believer 8:1,2
- Because of this, all that God has done on our behalf, we present our bodies daily as living sacrifices by the renewing of our minds to serve God – our only reasonable response 12:1,2.

The Old Testament promise fulfilled Paul's detailed knowledge of the Old Testament and the Jewish faith allowed him to crystallize these truths in simple language.

There are many references to the Old Testament – we must remember it was the Bible of their day.

Relevance of the Epistles of Paul

The Epistles written by the apostle Paul to the early churches are particularly important because for a number of reasons they confirm the doctrine of the early church -

- Paul was a contemporary of the first disciples
- He was a Pharisee and was antagonistic to the teachings of Jesus to the extent that he persecuted believers
- He became a dedicated and zealous follower of Jesus
- Being an expert in the Scriptures he could explain the relevance and importance of the Old Testament to the Gospel of Jesus Christ in the light of his new revelation
- His letters are the earliest available record of the church
- Some of the letters were written within twenty five years of the resurrection - Galatians was written in AD 49; Corinthians and Thessalonians by AD 56 and Romans in AD 57
- The Synoptic Gospels were not written till around AD 60
- The letters show the teaching of the first believers
- Paul's understanding came from direct revelation of Jesus without detailed influence of the other disciples

- The teaching of Paul may be compared and is compatible with the teaching of Peter as outlined in the Acts of the Apostles
- The Gospels do not show dependence on the letters of Paul.

SUMMARY
The Gospel is the Power of God 1:1-32
The Righteous Judgment of God 2:1 to 3:31
God's Plan of Salvation 3:21-31
Justification by Faith 4:1-25
Peace and Joy through the Holy Spirit 5:1 to 8:39
The Sovereignty of God 9:1 to 11:36
Our Response as Living Sacrifices 12:1,2
Kingdom Conduct 12:3 to 15:12
Paul's Ministry to the Gentiles 15:14 to 16:27

THE GOSPEL IS THE POWER OF GOD
1:1,2 The Gospel is the Good News of forgiveness of sin and of eternal salvation. It was promised by God in the Old Testament Is 53:12.

1:3-4 Son of God The Gospel is centered on God's Son Jesus Christ our Lord -
- He is descended from David by human nature v3
- He is declared with power to be the Son of God as evidenced by the miracles and healings he performed
- He demonstrated his Sonship by the Spirit of holiness - his sinless life and the evidence of the Holy Spirit working through him v4
- His death on the cross was confirmed as acceptance for the forgiveness of sins as shown by his resurrection from the dead Acts 24:14,15; 26:6-8. The need for his death shows the awfulness of sin and the worth of the soul to God
- Paul refers to Jesus as the Son of God in most of his letters 1Cor 1:9; 2Cor 1:19; Gal 2:20; Eph 1:3.

1:5 *The obedience that comes from faith* refers to the desire that is in the heart of the born again believer to live by God's Word empowered by the indwelling presence of the Holy Spirit.

1:6-7 *Those who are called to belong to Jesus Christ* *v6* Believers are called **saints** – set apart for his service - called, chosen from before the foundation of the world, to be holy and blameless in his sight, by God's grace, not their deeds Eph 1:4.

1:7 **Deity of the Son** Jesus is included with God the Father in the promise of grace and peace confirming his deity.

1:8-10 **Prayer** is an important part of ministry, both to pray for others and to pray for the activities we undertake.

1:11,12 **Mutual ministry** occurs between those who work together as we receive from each other. We must recognize our gifts from God and our responsibility as individuals to minister to those amongst whom we serve especially to encourage.

1:13 Despite his best intentions Paul only got to Rome under house arrest.

1:14,15 **Our Obligation** Paul was eager to share at all times. We each have a duty to tell others about Jesus.

1:16,17 **The Gospel** is the means God has provided by which a person can be accepted as righteous in his presence. We should not be ashamed to testify.

It is based on faith from beginning to end It is not earned by good deeds but imputed, given by God's free grace - and applies to a person of any nation who believes in Jesus as Savior and Lord. The Gospel is the focus of these chapters.

1:18-20 **The Problem of Holiness and Sin** The eternal God has revealed himself as holy. He created mankind for fellowship and to live by his ways which reveal his character and are best for us Lev 11:45. From the beginning man chose to be independent from God Gen 3:22. God cannot condone sin - judgment comes on those who turn away from him Gen 6:6-8.

Knowledge of the Creator There are three ways in which God has made himself known -

• **Natural Knowledge** God who is Spirit has made known **his invisible qualities - his eternal power and divine nature - his sovereignty and glory** are clearly displayed in all that he has created Ps 19:1-14. This includes the marvels discovered by natural science which confirm the intelligence and purpose behind the physical universe and the human body.

• **Revelation** The presence and purpose of God have been revealed throughout the generations to countless individuals and as recorded in the Word of God. This revelation has been more particularly demonstrated in the life, death and resurrection of Jesus Christ as also contained in the Scriptures

- **Personal Awareness in the human heart** We all bear God's image Gen 1:26,27. God has revealed **his divine nature and character** within the heart of every person. We all have a sense of what is right and wrong especially in regard to our own welfare Ecc 3:11. We hold people accountable who transgress our sense of moral acceptance and expect justice for ourselves.

1:20 **We are without excuse** Because of this clear evidence of God's presence, people have no excuse when they willfully ignore God and deny him.

1:21-23 **The Response** Many refuse to acknowledge God. The Word of God declares that *they knew God v21.* Yet they claim to be wise by living independent from him - this is the great offense Is 29:16. They worship the creation, created beings and possessions rather than the immortal God Ps 14:1. They idolize people and deny the One who gives life and all things. They see the creation as having occurred by chance and for no purpose - human life and 'self' as originating from nothing through a mindless progression of cells without reason and destined for extinction.

1:24-32 **The Consequence of Unbelief** Many people turn from God and become self-centered, living for their own interests. So God gives such people over to follow their own desires. They must suffer the consequences of their wrongdoing. They not only do evil things but approve those who do them.

THE RIGHTEOUS JUDGMENT OF GOD

2:1-5 **The Moral Order** We quickly pass judgment on those who do wrong against us – we require a standard for ourselves v3. That sense of justice confirms that there will be a time when God will require each person to give account of their thoughts, words and actions v6. Our sense of justice demands it.

2:6,7 **Those who acknowledge God and follow his ways** When the time of accountability comes those who have chosen to seek God and do good can expect *glory, honor and immortality - and eternal life Jn 3:16.*

2:8-11 **Those who reject the truth** Those who deny God and are self-seeking will experience anger, wrath and separation – the outworking of justice. This will occur in the last day when each person is called to account by the **'book of deeds'** v16. The alternative is have one's name recorded in the **'Lambs Book of Life'** Rev 20:11-15.

2:12-17 **The Standard** The standard of acceptance will be God's law which is based on his nature and character. Those who do not know God's law will be measured by the law which is within themselves *written on their hearts v14,15.*

2:17-29 **Those who know the law** Judgment will not be based on worldly standards, outward ceremony and human recognition. It will be by thoughts, words and actions - *of the heart, by the Spirit, not by the written code v29;* Jer 17:9,10; Mt 12:35-37.

No One is Righteous – not even one!

3:1-20 The Jewish people thought they had an advantage because they had received the Ten Commandments through Moses on Mt Sinai. But God's Law had to be applied - from the heart. This they failed to do. As God's holy nature determines the requirements of the law including justice, love and mercy, justice also demands that all the conditions of the law be met at all times. History confirms that this has not been achieved v10-19. It is clear that *no one will be declared righteous in his sight by observing the law v20.* We cannot come up to the standard required by God's nature because of the natural tendency to do what is wrong. This is 'original sin' and affects every person because of Adam's fall Gen 3:22. Paul knew the burden of trying to earn forgiveness and salvation through one's own efforts and merit, as required by other belief systems and philosophies of mankind. He found that deeds could never remove guilt or punishment and have no benefit for the dead. Works might give personal release but do not draw closer to God. *Through the law we become conscious of sin v20.*

Righteousness from God

3:21,22 How could the holy God bring fallen mankind into a state of acceptance in his presence?

Righteousness means having the right to stand in the presence of God without offense, charge or guilt. As no one could maintain the standard determined by his nature, God in his mercy provided another way for a person to receive his righteousness.

This righteousness from God comes through faith in Jesus Christ to all who believe v22 - to those who accept his death as payment for their sins 6:23. *God made him who had no sin to be sin for us, so that in him we might become the righteousness of God 2Cor 5:21.*

Jesus took our place in judgment – as a sinner – so that we might stand in his place, in right standing before God Rom 5:8.

GOD'S PLAN OF SALVATION

It is important to identify key points and verses and commit them to memory so we may be able to share them with others.

3:23-31 **We understand that -**
- *all have sinned and fall short of the glory of God v23*
- *the wages of sin is death but the gift of God is eternal life – in Christ Jesus our Lord 6:23*
- **we** *are justified freely by his grace - through the redemption that came by Christ v24* - we cannot save ourselves Eph 2:8,9
- **God allowed Jesus to become** *a sacrifice of atonement through faith in his blood v25* - by dying on the cross in our place, as a perfect sacrifice, Jesus paid the penalty of our sin and **removed the offense of our sin before God**
- **when we accept Jesus as Savior and Lord we receive righteousness from God** v22 – it is imputed to us by God's grace, not earned by our efforts or good deeds 1:17
- **as a result we are born again through faith in Jesus** v26; Jn 1:12,13 – this takes place by the operation of the Holy Spirit.

God's holiness & righteous justice were satisfied - his mercy and love were demonstrated - they came together on the cross! 5:8.

Justification means to be deemed to be without charge, without guilt, acquitted, absolved - 'just-as-if' I had never sinned! v24 – to be able to stand *faultless before the presence of his glory with exceeding joy Jude 1:24.*

Grace means free, unlimited, unmerited, favor that is not deserved and cannot be earned - it is not based on the one who receives or on the response - it is based entirely on the nature and character of the Giver v24 Eph 2:8,9.

Redemption means to be delivered from debt – purchased back to the rightful owner. Jesus paid a debt he did not owe - my debt I could not pay.

Atonement means to remove the offense of sin before God so that the offender can be cleansed and become at one with God – to be reconciled with God. The mercy of God has obliterated the certificate of debt incurred by breaking the law that was against us Col 2:13,14 – this was the triumph of the cross that set us free from the penalty and power of sin Mic 7:19; Acts 3:19.

Through faith in his blood – This salvation has been made available by God through the shed blood of Jesus and is appropriated by the believer through faith in Jesus – by accepting him as Savior and Lord v22,25,26.

JUSTIFICATION BY FAITH

4:1-17 **Abraham was justified by faith** – by what he believed and not by what he did v3. He lived in a polytheistic culture. When called by God he responded by leaving home and went to the land to which he was directed. When told by God that he would have a son in his old age *Abraham believed the LORD and he credited it to him as righteousness Gen 15:6.* This demonstrated the principle that God wants us to believe what he tells us. Abraham eventually had a son, Isaac, so he received the promise through faith. In the same way we receive **God's gift of righteousness** when we believe in Jesus as our Savior and Lord. So Abraham became the 'father of faith' to all who believe v16.

4:18,19 **Believing Faith** Our faith is genuine when we believe that God will do what he has promised - *when all reason for hope was gone Abraham continued to hope v18.*
This is the example for us to follow -
• in regard to our salvation - we are saved by believing Jn 1:12
• in the way in which we respond to the way God tells us to live and in the things he leads us to do Jn 14:15
• in the way we receive the promises in his Word 10:10.

4:20-25 **Righteousness through believing -**
• no distrust made him waver regarding the promise of God v20
• he grew strong in his faith as he gave glory to God v20
• fully convinced that God was able to do what he had promised v21
• this is why *it was credited to him as righteousness v22.*

PEACE and JOY THROUGH THE HOLY SPIRIT

The joy of knowing Jesus - There are those who believe that science reduces everything to a materialistic world. The five senses used to investigate physical phenomenon are only half the human being – they ignore experience and spiritual perception. The disciples had a personal involvement with Jesus but they could not understand his references to death and rising again – it was outside their field of experience Mt 20:19; Mk 8:31; Lk 24:46; Jn 20:9. After the resurrection their lives were transformed by the encounter with the risen Lord. It is this relationship with the risen Lord Jesus Christ that believers enter into when they acknowledge him as Savior and Lord. They experience a whole new dimension of living that impacts all areas of existence and changes every circumstance.

5:1-4 **We have peace with God** Therefore (because right standing with God comes through faith in Christ alone) we have a new relationship with God through faith in Christ - we are **reconciled** with God. We have a new hope of seeing and sharing the glory of God v2. This causes us to be filled with joy. We even experience joy in suffering because we know its purpose – to produce perseverance, character and increased hope v3,4.

5:5 **We also experience the presence of the Holy Spirit** by whom God has poured out his love into our hearts.

5:6-8 **God demonstrates his love for us in this** – while we were still sinners, Christ died for us. We can love now, not in our own strength but through God's love which is poured out into our hearts, which fills us and overflows through us!

5:9-11 **Reconciled with God** – brought back into relationship, harmony - the offense of our sin has been removed by Jesus – the consequence of the atonement v11; 3:23-31; 2Cor 5:17-21.

5:12-17 **The significance of Adam** It is important to understand that the Creation record in the first three chapters of Genesis reveals three truths –
• God created and sustains the universe
• Mankind departed from the unique position in the plan of God through disobedience and as a result human nature now falls short of God's nature
• There is a need for mankind to be reconciled with God.
However we may see the Genesis creation account recorded some 4,000 years ago in comparison with current scientific discoveries and knowledge we must recognize the significance of this revelation. These timeless truths could be understood by the people of the day and are equally clear today to those who are prepared to consider them. No other philosophy or worldview explains the fallen state of human nature.
We were all affected by 'original sin' because of Adam's independence from God – sin entered human nature through Adam. With this came mortality and eventual judgment Gen 3:22. As the disobedience of one man Adam brought separation from God for all mankind so the obedience of one man Jesus Christ brought reconciliation and eternal life for all those who will place their trust in him v12-15.
There was a cosmic change in the world order when Jesus died on the cross v17. The legal requirements of the law have been met 3:25,26. Relationship with God has been restored. Through faith in Jesus Christ

we can enter a new era of grace, righteousness and abundant life Jn 10:10. No other philosophy offers the promise of eternal life.

5:17-22 We reign in life through Jesus The great need of the individual is to find the means to live the life they know they should. Many are overcome by the circumstances of life and struggle to find fulfilment. The born again believer finds a new resource that overcomes the world - that the words of Jesus are true – *streams of living water will flow from within Jn 7:37-39.*

6:1-18 New life in Christ Just as Jesus rose from the dead, in the same way the believer is raised to new life through faith in him. When Jesus died on the cross the power of sin was broken so *that we should no longer be slaves to sin v6.* We have taken part symbolically with him in his death so we are made alive spiritually to God through his resurrection v8.

We need to know this – *count yourselves dead to sin but alive to God in Christ Jesus v11.* We do not offer our body to sin but offer ourselves to God because sin is no longer our master - we no longer have to sin v13.

6:19-23 Set free to serve God We have been released from sin to serve God - the result is eternal life - *the gift of God is eternal life in Christ Jesus our Lord v23.*

7:1-25 We now belong to Jesus In the example of marriage the woman is bound to her husband while he is alive. When he dies the woman is set free to remarry. We have died to the old way of satisfying the physical flesh so that we might belong to Christ to serve in the new way of the Spirit v4-6.

The law shows us the nature of God but we could not keep all the requirements of the law. We have the desire to do what is good but find we cannot always do it.

So there are three principles (laws) at work in us and for us –

• Law 1 - The desire in our inner being wants to obey God's law and do what we know is right v22

• Law 2 - The evil intention within our members draws us away from what we want to do – the law of sin and death v23

This results in continual ongoing struggle.

Thanks be to God - through Jesus Christ our Lord - there is a third principle - available through faith in Christ v25 -

• Law 3 - The Law of the Spirit of life in Christ Jesus 8:1,2.

8:1-11 Life through the Holy Spirit There is now no condemnation for the person who has accepted Jesus as Savior and Lord – no condemnation for anything or from anyone! Jesus made the Law of the Spirit of life available by his death on the cross and the sending of the Holy Spirit to live within the believer. This law of the Spirit sets the believer free from the other law – the law that brings death through the inability to obey all of God's requirements. Law 3 works in us when we live according to the leading of the Holy Spirit v4. We set our minds on what the Holy Spirit wants rather than on what our sinful human nature wants. We follow the leading of the Holy Spirit and he gives us the power to live the new life v9-11.

8:12-17 You must be born again The new birth occurs when we receive Jesus as Savior and Lord. The Spirit within us brings this about and also confirms that we have actually been born again – that we are **children of God** v14; Jn 1:12,13; 3:3-8. Because of this we are also co-heirs with Christ, even if we suffer persecution, for we will also share his glory v14-17.

8:18-25 Sharing God's glory The whole creation is looking forward to the return of Jesus Christ when **God's Plan of Salvation** will be fulfilled and all things will be made new v22; 3:21-31. We long for that day and the Holy Spirit helps us as we work towards it v26.

8:26,27 Help when we pray We don't know what is best for ourselves or for others so the Spirit helps us in our weakness - he intercedes, presenting our prayers and needs to God. This is great encouragement for us when we feel we don't know what or how to pray - the Holy Spirit takes our best efforts and deepest sighs and presents them acceptably before the Father.

8:28-30 *We know that in all things God works for the good of those who love him* v28 We can be confident that God works out every step of his plan – he foreknew us, predestined, called, justified and glorified us v29,30; Eph 1:4-8. Our circumstances are arranged by God to prepare us for the calling he has planned us for. It took forty years of solitude for Moses to learn that God's ways are not the ways of the world Acts 7:22-30.

8:31-39 We are more than conquerors God has done everything to secure our future - we have nothing to fear v31. As well as this Jesus who will judge all mankind intercedes for us at the right hand of God.

Nothing - *will be able to separate us from the love of God that is in Christ Jesus our Lord v38.*

THE SOVEREIGNTY OF GOD

Having presented the truths of what God has done for us in Christ Jesus the need for personal response is outlined.

Two great truths are revealed in the Scriptures – the Sovereignty of God and the Freewill of the individual. That God is sovereign over all creation is indisputable. He is the absolute good. At the same time God has given us the ability to choose, between good and evil, between right and wrong, between relationship and rebellion. This freedom brings with it responsibility for our decisions and actions for which we will be held accountable – our sense of justice demands it. While this may be difficult for some to accept, the limitations of the human mind sometimes prevent us from coming closer than recognizing that there are two principles that appear to conflict where both are supported by Scripture – this is known as an antinomy Is 55:8,9.

9:1-33 God's election Abraham was chosen to receive God's revelation about faith. But not all the descendants of Abraham were included in the promise. Isaac was chosen over Ishmael, Jacob was chosen over Esau. God's purpose in election stands not by works but by God's sovereign choice v11. It is not based on man's desire or effort but on God's mercy v16. God raised up Pharaoh in the days of Moses *that I might display my power in you and that my name might be proclaimed in all the earth v17.*

This principle of sovereignty and responsibility is also evident in the life of Joseph and recognized by him - *you intended to harm me, but God intended it for good to accomplish what is now being done, the saving of many lives Gen 4:20.*

God has mercy on some and hardens others v18. While this is a mystery it demonstrates both God's sovereign power and the glory of his mercy v23. This is also shown in his choosing the Gentiles to participate with Israel in his salvation plan v24. Acceptance in the eternal kingdom will be, not by works, but by faith and trust in Christ alone v30:33; Acts 9:1-19.

10:1-21 Faith comes by believing God Moses explained that to become righteousness it was necessary to meet all the requirements of the law at all times. This proved to be impossible. God had already provided a second way of obtaining righteousness – **a righteousness that is received by faith**.

This righteousness requires that we believe what God says 1:17 –

• **we have God's Word** – we must believe it and speak it. If we **confess** 'Jesus is Lord' and **believe** in our hearts that God has raised him from the dead we will be saved v8,9

• we **believe** this in our hearts and **express** it in our lives. This is how God's power is outworked in us – through **faith** followed by **believing response** v10

• faith comes from hearing God's Word through Jesus Christ and believing it – responding to it v17; Heb 11:6

• so as we read God's Word and believe it our faith develops – all the miracles of Jesus were in response to faith Mt 8:5-13

• we believe all of God's promises which are available to us and see them outworked in our lives through faith.

Receiving God's promises This is how all of God's promises are received. We know what God has promised in his Word, we believe it in our heart, we express it on our lips and then patiently outwork it until we see it fulfilled! We may hear or read what God says but until we actually believe it and put it into action in our lives we only have head knowledge without faith.

11:1-24 **The Remnant of Israel** The people of Israel were God's chosen people for almost 2,000 years. With the coming of Jesus the Messiah through the Jewish people God was not rejecting his people but opening the way for people of all nations to be included in his plan of salvation v11.

God's people failed because of unbelief – their trial was prophesied Deu 28:25; Jer 24:9; Hos 9:17.

We stand by faith v20,25. Many Jewish people have since come to faith in Jesus Christ accepting him as the Messiah.

The day is coming when the remnant of Israel will be saved by faith v26. As foretold by the prophets there are many unfulfilled promises in the Old Testament which will be outworked in the last days Is 59:20; Jer 31:33-34; Ezk 34:23; Dan 7:13,14.

11:28-32 **God's gifts and call are irrevocable** All the promises of God have their confirmation in Jesus Christ 2Cor 1:20. While this applies to the remnant of Israel it also includes God's promise of eternal life and

13

all the promises of Jesus to be with us and use us in the extension of his kingdom v29.

God's mercy extends to all who will acknowledge him and follow his ways v32.

11:33-36 **The unsearchable wisdom of God** – these revealed truths are beyond our detailed understanding but bring joy and awe, gratitude and humility to the heart of the believer as we contemplate the glory and mercy of God Is 40:13.

There are those who would fashion God to fit within the limitations of the human mind. We must rather let our minds and hearts expand to begin to appreciate and appropriate the grandeur of the Creator, Sustainer and Provider and to embrace the joy that comes through a growing personal relationship with him. He has given us all that we have and are – our life, abilities, locations, families, provisions and situations v36.

OUR RESPONSE AS LIVING SACRIFICES

12:1,2 These two verses are pivotal in understanding and applying the principles of the message of Romans.

The first eleven chapters describe **what God has done for us in Christ** – forgiveness, salvation, new life and an eternal future.

The last four chapters define **our reasonable response in the way we choose to live our lives.**

- *Therefore* – because of what God has done for us in Christ
- *I urge you* – an important matter that requires urgent and immediate action by each one of us
- *in view of God's mercy* – we can only achieve this because of God's great mercy to us and operating within us
- *to offer your bodies as living sacrifices* – our bodies represent all of us - mind, heart, activities, time, resources – our five senses - we give our body to God and he allows us to go on living for him – this requires a conscious decision
- *holy and pleasing to God* – we are each acceptable just as we are - this is our position because of what Jesus did by dying in our place to remove the offence of our sin
- *this is your spiritual act of worship* – the only reasonable response in view of God's great goodness and mercy.

How do we do this?

• *Do not be conformed any longer to the pattern of the world* – the world is against God and Jesus - we conform (look like the world) by taking in the inputs from the world – media, peer influence, entertainment and worldly standards

• *but be transformed by the renewing of your mind* – as our mind is conditioned by the inputs from the world so now we focus on the inputs from the Word of God. The Holy Spirit transforms us, step by step into God's likeness 2Cor 3:16-18

• *Then you will be able to test and approve what God's will is - his good pleasing and perfect will* for your life – as we give ourselves to God and focus on his Word he leads us in the best way to live our lives.

KINGDOM CONDUCT

Having responded to Jesus as Savior and Lord the remaining chapters give guidelines on how we are to live pleasing to God as we take on his nature – the process of sanctification.

12:3-8 **We belong to the other believers** The foundation for service is humility, understanding that all we are and all we have comes from God through Christ. We belong to the **'body' of believers** and each member must freely use their differing gifts and abilities for the building up of others - prophesying, serving, teaching, encouraging, contributing, leadership and showing mercy – these are just some of the gifts of the Holy Spirit given for ministering to others Eph 4:11; 1Cor 12:7-11.

12:9-21 **The way of love** God's love is poured out in our hearts so we can love others sincerely, with devotion and humility 5:5. As we serve we never lack in zeal, we keep our spiritual fervor and enthusiasm through the Holy Spirit – this comes from a close relationship with the Lord. We learn always to be joyful in hope, patient, faithful in prayer and generous v13.

We are children of the blessing v14; Gal 3:14; Eph 1:3 We receive every blessing from God which we can pass on to others and so we should.

We have consideration for others and are not proud or conceited.

We do not take revenge or pursue evil but overcome evil by doing good v21.

13:1-10 **Respect for authority** All authority has been put in place by God. We should be model citizens obeying the law, supporting our leaders and praying for them. They are appointed to provide our security. Pay taxes and outstanding debts.

Follow the spirit of the law as taught by Jesus – love is the fulfilment of the law Mt 22: 37-40; Jn 13:34,35.

13:11-14 **Clothe yourself with Jesus** We know the time for the return of Jesus is near. So rather than conforming to the ways of the world we clothe ourselves with the Lord Jesus Christ – take on his nature. We act as Jesus would and should ask in each situation 'what would Jesus have me do?' - rather than thinking about how to gratify the desires of the sinful nature.

14:1-9 **Freedom and responsibility** We have been set free by our relationship with Christ. But we should always think about the faith and wellbeing of others. We must work out what is right for us but we must also not cause offense to others who are members of the same body – we each belong to the Lord.

14:10-12 **The judgment seat** We will each stand before God's judgment seat and give an account to God 2Cor 5:10. Thankfully we have Christ who has gained our salvation and eternal life. Yet we must be responsible before God for those he leads across our path, to share the Gospel and help them where we can.

14:13-23 **Mutual edification** We need to recognize that *the kingdom of God is - about righteousness, peace and joy in the Holy Spirit v17* - it is not about what we eat or drink. We make every effort to do what leads to peace and mutual edification. We are blessed when we stand before Christ with a clear conscience. But if we have doubts we should refrain from acting because everything that is not done from and in faith is sin v23.

15:1-3 **Personal ministry** Those who are strong in the faith must not only please themselves but look to help in building up others especially those weaker in faith. This is the example set by Jesus and brings joy and blessing in service v3; Jn 13:12-17.

15:4 **The Word of God is our guide** Everything contained in God's Word is there to teach us and to give us encouragement, perseverance and hope in every situation Jn 5:39; 1Cor 10:11.

15:5-12 **A spirit of unity** As we apply the Word to our lives we experience a common focus and a spirit of unity with other believers so that with one heart and mouth we will bring glory to God the Father and the Lord Jesus Eph 4:1-3. He came to confirm the promises God made to the patriarchs because as a result of his death and resurrection they now apply to us! v7; Jn 5:39. As believers we need to put aside our minor discrepancies and work together to give the people of the world every opportunity to respond to the Gospel of Jesus.

THE GOD OF HOPE

15:13 This verse describes how we receive the continual blessedness available to the one who believes in Jesus -
- *The God of Hope* – God is the source and means of all hope
- *fill you* – God wants to fill us to the brim with ALL joy and peace – the fullness of his presence
- *as you trust in him* – as we continue to activate our faith by daily reading his Word and walking with Jesus, responding to the leading of his Holy Spirit
- *so that you may overflow with hope* – God will fill us because he wants us to overflow with expectation of his goodness and power outworking in our lives and in the things he calls us to do
- *by the power of the Holy Spirit* – this is achieved by the indwelling presence of the Holy Spirit Acts 1:8.

This blessedness only comes as we put our belief into practice in our daily lives Ps 89:15-19; Eph 4:18-21.

PAUL'S MINISTRY TO THE GENTILES

15:14-16 **Our priestly duty** Paul was given the priestly duty specifically of presenting the Gospel to the Gentiles (non Jews) Acts 9:15,16. It is the wonder of the wisdom and mercy of God that he should choose an antagonistic Pharisee to take the message of the Messiah to the non-Jewish people. No clearer evidence could be given of the reality of Paul's calling.

Sanctified - means to be set apart, for a special purpose, to be made holy v16. We are sanctified by the Holy Spirit. This is an ongoing process that begins when we are born again and will be completed when we see Jesus and will be like him 1Cor 15:49.

15:17-22 **I glory in Christ Jesus** Paul was motivated to talk only about the things that have been achieved by him through the power of the Holy Spirit in his ministry v17,19. He had preached from Jerusalem to the whole of Asia Minor and into Macedonia and Greece preferring to speak to those who had never heard v20-22. We each have a priestly duty 1Pet 2:9.

15:23-29 Ministry in Jerusalem, Rome and Spain He now planned to visit Rome, the center of the Roman Empire and then to go on to Spain after returning to Jerusalem with gifts for the poor. It is recorded that he actually achieved these goals.

The believers (saints) in Jerusalem were in need perhaps due to being a minority in a capital city. Paul collected gifts from the Gentile believers which he would personally take to Jerusalem 1Cor 16:1-4; 2Cor 8:1-7; 9:1-5. This was a major reason for the return to Jerusalem Acts 24:17.

15:30-33 Importance of prayer Paul again emphasized the importance of prayer both for himself and for the success of the ministry. We neglect prayer for ministry and missionaries because of our doubts about effectiveness. Paul had no such doubts - he prayed continually and encouraged others to do the same 1:8-10. He saw that the regular prayers of the believers at home were a vital part of the whole ministry!

Greetings to the Believers in Rome

16:1-16 The Body of Christ The church community in Rome was well established before Paul's pending visit perhaps by visitors who were present at Pentecost Acts 2:5 and even included members of Caesar's household Phil 4:22. Many of them met in home groups, some led by women whom Paul commended for their ministries. Most were known personally to him and some had been lead to the Lord by him. There is no mention of Peter in Rome at this time as his predominant leadership role was in Jerusalem and subsequently in Asia.

16:17-19 Divisions and Obstacles The church has always been hindered by the divisions caused by self-centered people and exertive personalities. The world is desperate for a unified body of believers with the pure message of salvation - a choice between heaven and hell rather than a plethora of divided churches. It is our responsibility to work together, in unity, with every other believer to present the good news of salvation through Jesus to the people - *for there the Lord bestows his blessing, even life forevermore Ps 133:1-3*; Eph 4:3.

16:20 Satan has been defeated by the death of Christ on the cross - his power over us is broken. As we continue to persevere with our service for Jesus we can be assured that God will crush the devil under our feet.

16:21-23 The Ministry Team Paul was always surrounded by a group of disciples, receiving instruction and training.

16:24 May the grace of our Lord Jesus Christ be with all of you - may we also be constantly aware of and proclaim the grace of God in Jesus.

16:25-27 **Gospel Summary – A cause for praise!**
God is able to secure the eternal future of those who believe -
• because of the selfless, sacrificial death of Jesus on the cross
• this was a mystery hidden from the beginning but now revealed
• it is made known from the prophetic Books through the Holy Spirit by the command of God Acts 28:23.
• so that anyone from all nations of the world might believe and obey him and receive eternal life!

Pursuit of godliness Paul's teaching to obey Jesus refutes the claim that he disregarded the law. He saw that the believer was released from the law in order to live a godly life by following Christ 1Tim 6:11; Tit 1:1.

Paul in Rome The aim of visiting Rome was achieved when Paul was arrested for being a cause of disturbance in Jerusalem. He appealed to be tried under Caesar as a Roman citizen and spent two years in house arrest AD 60-62 where he continued to proclaim the Gospel freely Acts 21:33; 25:10-12; 28:30,31.

After his release due to lack of charge he is believed to have made a number of mission visits as recorded in the Epistles – to Ephesus and Macedonia 1Tim 1:3; Crete Tit 1:5; Nicopolis Tit 3:12; Colosse Phm 1:22 and possibly Spain 15:24,25.

He returned to Rome under arrest and was martyred (beheaded as a Roman citizen) under Nero AD 67.

His time in Rome and his contribution to the church in Rome is recognized as equal with that of Peter by the early Christian writers.

Death of Christ

The death of Jesus on the cross is central and fundamental to the message of the Gospel – the object of his coming was to give his life a ransom for many Mt 20:28.

1. The Nature of God - God is holy, separate, absolute in being, wisdom, power, justice, goodness, moral excellence and ethical perfection – free from limitation, embracing all the attributes of perfection (glory) 1Sam 2:2; Ps 99:5; Is 6:1-3; Rev 4:8.

As such God requires holiness in his people – be holy, because I am holy Lev 19:2; Is 57:15; 1Pet 1:15,16.

God's nature is revealed in the moral order of the universe. Justice requires conformity or separation.

2. The Nature of Mankind - Mankind was made in the image of God in a perfect environment with eternal perspective Gen 1:26,27. Mankind has fallen from that privileged position through the desire for independence Gen 3:22.

Sin means falling short of the glory of God Rom 3:23 - doing, saying or thinking what is not in conformity with the nature of God as described in his Word Mt 12:35,36. The human heart is inclined to sin Jer 17:9. The result of sin is a sense of guilt, condemnation and alienation from God.

Because of the fallen nature it is difficult for the natural person to see the terrible offense of sin to God as revealed by the need for the death of God's Son. Nor can they understand the need of salvation Jer 44:4; Rom 8:7,8; Eph 2:1-3.

Conviction of sin is needed to seek the glory of God.

3. The Penalty of sin - Every legal system has a penalty which must apply. Sin is an offense to the holiness of God Hab 1:13. The consequence of sin is separation from God – the wages of sin is death Rom 6:23. Ultimately this is the condition for eternity 2Thes 1:8-10. It is only as one comes to consider the greatness of God that the awfulness of sin and the desperate condition of mankind are recognized Ps 8:1-9; 19:1-14.

Without holiness no one will see the Lord Heb 12:14.

4. Sacrifice for sin - It was God's eternal purpose that mankind should return to fellowship with him 2Pet 3:9; Rev 21:3; Eph 3:11. We could not fulfill the requirements of God's Nature. Only God could intervene –

• A sacrifice shows the seriousness of the offense and the genuineness of the repentance. It requires a precious offering in place of the guilty party – *and without the shedding of blood there is no forgiveness Heb 9:22*

• It was necessary that the offense of sin be removed and the penalty paid by a perfect, sinless sacrifice. Jesus paid the price and bore the penalty due to us – *who loved us and gave himself for us an offering and a sacrifice to God Eph 5:2*; 1Jn 3:5

• He became a substitute, a vicarious sufferer – he died in place of the sinner – *Christ died for us Rom 5:6-8;* 1Cor 15:3; 1Thes 5:10; 1Pet 2:24

• Jesus had to be made like us so as to fulfill the requirements of the law, then destroy death and the evil one and make atonement for the sins of the people Heb 2:14-17. He fulfilled the Old Testament principle of sacrifice Is 53:4-6; 1Jn 3:8

Passover was a sacrifice to the Lord – death passed over the people, as they were delivered from slavery in Egypt Ex 12:27 – Jesus is *The Lamb of God who takes away the sin of the world Jn 1:29; Christ our Passover is sacrificed for us 1Cor 5:7; the Lamb that was slain from the creation of the world Rev 13:8.*

5. Atonement - means to remove the offense of sin before God so that the offender can be cleansed and become at one with God, back in harmony – reconciled with God Rom 5:11 -

• **Expiation** – means to make up for, by repayment, accepting punishment. Jesus paid the penalty of sin, satisfying the just demands of the Law (God's moral nature) - *God made him who had no sin to be sin for us, so that in him we might become the righteousness of God 2Cor 5:21*

• **Propitiation** – means to make favorable, by removing the stain of sin – to put mankind right – God sent his Son *the atoning sacrifice for our sins 1Jn 2:2; 4:10.*

Atonement must be seen from God's side - as in all things God initiated the atonement – *God was reconciling the world to himself in Christ, not counting men's sins against them 2Cor 5:19.*

• The legal requirements of the Law have been met by Jesus - *God presented him as a sacrifice of atonement, through faith in his blood – he did it to demonstrate his justice – so as to be just and the one who justifies those who have faith in Jesus Rom 3:25,26*

• Appeasement of God's displeasure and wrath was achieved by meeting the just demands of the Law by a willing sacrifice of infinite worth – his holy and righteous nature was vindicated Rom 3:25; 1Jn 2:2; 4:10

- God's righteous justice and holiness have been satisfied by the perfect obedience and voluntary death of Christ on the cross – the penalty paid, the offense removed Heb 9:11-15
- God's unconditional love, mercy and grace are demonstrated in the forgiveness of sin Rom 5:8; Eph 1:7 – *this is my blood of the new covenant which is poured out for many for the forgiveness of sins Mt 26:28*
- The mercy and wisdom of God has obliterated the certificate of debt incurred by breaking the law that was against us Col 2:13,14 – this was the triumph of the cross that set us free from the penalty and power of sin Mic 7:19; Acts 3:19.

6. Reconciliation – means the removal of the separation and enmity caused by sin and the restoration of man to right relationship and fellowship with God – this was achieved by the atonement 2Cor 5:18-21. *Christ died for us – we have now been justified by his blood – saved from God's wrath - through whom we have now received reconciliation Rom 5:8-11. Christ also has once suffered for sins, the just for the unjust, that he might bring us to God 1Pet 3:18.* He freed us from our sin by his own blood 1Pet 1:19,20; Rev 1:5,6; 13:8.

- **Redemption** – to recover – to buy back to the rightful owner - to be delivered from debt, purchased 1Cor 7:23. We have been rescued from slavery, bondage to sin and death – a slave set free – by the blood of Jesus 1Pet 1:18; Rom 3:21-24; Eph 1:7; Heb 10:4. Jesus paid a debt he did not owe - my debt I could not pay.
- **Ransom -** *The death of Christ paid the price of the penalty for sin - For there is one God and one mediator between God and men, the man Christ Jesus, who gave himself as a ransom for all men 1Tim 2:5,6.* Mt 20:28.

7. Outcome - The restoration and fulfillment of God's purpose for creation was achieved by God's initiative when Jesus took our sin on himself and endured the punishment we deserve – death and separation from God.

- **Justification** – to be without charge, without guilt, acquitted, absolved - 'just-as-if' I had never sinned!

We are justified by his blood Rom 5:9 – to stand *faultless before the presence of his glory with exceeding joy Jude 1:24. He was delivered over to death for our sins and raised to life for our justification Rom 4:25*
- **Righteousness** is imputed – reckoned, credited – charged to our account Rom 1:16,17; 3:21-25; 4:3-11.

When we comprehend the holiness of God and the awfulness of separation we become eternally thankful to Jesus.

Adoption – we are taken into the family of God – the relationship is restored Rom 8:15; Eph 1:5. We receive all rights in the new family – having relinquished all rights of the past.

The cross also shows the incredible worth of the individual soul to God Jn 3:16.

We now have eternal life – the way to the tree of life has been reopened Gen 3:22-24; Rev 22:14. Jesus took on physical, human life so that the believer might have eternal life.

The whole object of the life of Jesus on earth was to reconcile man with God, both in this life and eternity Jn 17:21; Eph 2:22-22; 1Cor 15:28. No wonder the evil one seeks to denigrate the Word of God and the Person of Jesus Christ.

8. Sanctification – our response is to be like Jesus – *be perfect – as your heavenly Father is perfect Mt 5:48*. We are being made holy as we bide in him Gal 2:20; Phil 4:13; Heb 12:1-2.

Examples of God's nature are found in the Ten Commandments; the Sermon on the Mount Mt 5:1-16; love your neighbor as yourself Mt 22:36-40; in humility and in serving one another Mt 20:24-28; in the Fruit of the Spirit Gal 5:22,23.

9. Salvation through faith in his blood – This salvation has been made possible by the shed blood of Jesus and is appropriated by the believer through faith in Jesus as Savior and Lord Rom 3:21-26. Each person needs to respond to this great love 1Jn 3:1. The alternative is separation for eternity.

Salvation is now available for all who will receive it 1Jn 2:2 – but it must be accepted in faith by identifying with Christ crucified Jn 14:6; Acts 2:21.

It is a matter of choice – *to all who receive him – he gave the right to become children of God – born of God Jn 1:12,13.*

Death of Christ

1 Corinthians

Introduction – Corinth was the capital of the Roman province of Greece since 44 BC and was a prosperous cosmopolitan center. Paul visited with Silas and Timothy during his second mission journey AD 50-53 where he stayed for some eighteen months establishing the first group of believers in Greece Acts 18:1. On his third mission journey AD 54-57 while in Ephesus he received a letter and some reports from Corinth describing problems of conduct and practices which had developed since his departure 1:11; 7:1. He addressed these issues directly in this teaching letter which he sent with Timothy before planning to visit Corinth again himself 4:17,19; 16:5; 2Cor 13:1-3.

Author – Paul from Ephesus to believers in Corinth.

Period – Around AD 54 - most eye witnesses to the resurrection were still alive 15:6.

Theme – The Outworking of Spiritual Life The Corinthian believers were new in their faith and were still actively involved in the ways of their old lifestyle. This involved practices which were contrary to the teaching of Jesus. They included disunity, selfishness, segregation and immorality. They were also abusing spiritual gifts. There were fourteen issues, all of which are apparent in modern society. In each case Paul took them back to the basic principles. The central guideline for conduct is *I have become all things to all men so that by all means possible I might save some 9:22*.

This instruction to the Corinthian believers confirms the moral ethic introduced by Jesus and adopted by the early believers. It also demonstrates that Paul enforced this standard of conduct as a consequence of salvation by faith in Christ alone. This is in complete agreement with the teaching of James Jas 1:22.

SUMMARY
The Changed Life of the Believer 1:1 to 2:5
God's Secret Wisdom 2:6-16
Unity Among All Believers 3:1 to 4:21
High Standards of Conduct 5:1 to 11:34
Spiritual Gifts 12:1 to 14:40
The Gospel and the Resurrection 15:1 to 16:24

THE CHANGED LIFE OF THE BELIEVER

***1:1-3* Believers are sanctified in Christ Jesus** and called to be holy – they are also saints, a term which applies to all believers – set apart for God Eph 1:1.

Sanctification – being made holy - is imputed, given to us because of Jesus Rom 15:16. It is also the ongoing work of the Holy Spirit in the believer's life - as we grow, we are being changed to be like Christ 15:49; 2Cor 3:18.

1:4-9 Paul gave thanks for the evidence of God's grace in the changed lives of the believers – they were enriched in every way! They were also exercising spiritual gifts.

God - has called you into fellowship with his Son Jesus Christ our Lord through the Holy Spirit – this fellowship is the present daily experience that is available to the believer v9.

***1:10-17* Divisions in the Church** – *the first issue.* There were quarrels about teaching and personalities. The problems of false teaching and dominant personalities continue in all activities. There is only one Gospel message. We must follow Jesus and the Word of God – not people or words of human wisdom.

The Cross is the Power and Wisdom of God to Save

1:18-31 Many think the message of the cross is foolish and so reject it. Because human nature resists God in a desire for independence he has chosen the simplicity of the message of the cross as the means of eternal salvation. Others want a miraculous sign to confirm their belief. We must remember that the miraculous signs performed by Jesus did not influence the self-centered religious leaders. While they acknowledged the miracles they did not want to change their lifestyles Jn 11:45-48.

The message of the cross is open to all, both wise and lowly. No one can stand before God in his own right – it is only because God has made Christ *our righteousness, holiness and redemption* that we can stand v30.

***2:1-5* Jesus Christ and Him Crucified** Paul knew that the salvation of a soul is due to the work of the Holy Spirit. He always spoke about Jesus and the crucifixion. Because of this our witnessing must also be based solely about Jesus – not on wise and persuasive words. It is then that we see *a demonstration of the Spirit's power v4.* Our faith must rest completely and only on God's power. Then our weakness, fear and trembling will be used to great effect – *My grace is sufficient for you, for my power is made perfect in weakness 2Cor 12:7-10.*

GOD'S SECRET WISDOM

2:6-16 The Realm of the Holy Spirit The physical world is coming to an end 2Pet 3:7; Rev 21:1. God is Spirit and there is a world of the Spirit hidden from before time began Jn 4:23,24. The physical universe was created within the spiritual eternal world - we live in the unseen presence of God Acts 17:28. God's wisdom is hidden from the people of the physical world but is revealed to the believer by the Holy Spirit. When we accept Jesus as Savior and Lord we are born again into the spiritual eternal world. God gives his Holy Spirit who helps *us understand what God has freely given us v11,12.* The person who does not have the Spirit cannot understand these things and does not accept them v14 but the born again believer does understand them because *we have the mind of Christ v16.*

Actually the physical matter we know as our world is currently believed to be only four percent of the space we live in. The remainder is some twenty-three percent 'dark matter' and seventy-three percent 'dark energy' both of which are not understood by science.

UNITY AMONG ALL BELIEVERS

3:1-4 Reverting back to the problem of disunity 1:10 - the transformation of the believer's life by the power of the cross and the presence of the Holy Spirit produce unity among the brethren regardless of class, race or background. If unity is not present people are acting as worldly and not spiritual. Obedience to the Holy Spirit by the individual will maintain unity, humility and forbearance Eph 4:1-3. The cause of division within the Church today and within denominations is the desire for self-promotion and the absence of humility. This is responsible for much of the ineffectiveness of believers and the poor image of the Church in the eyes of the unbeliever Ps 133:1-3.

3:5-15 God makes the change in the life of a person - Regardless of human effort the changed life is God's work through the action of the Holy Spirit – *so neither he who plants nor he who waters is anything but only God who makes things grow v7.* For we are God's fellow workers! v9. We must each do our best to contribute to God's building - the body of believers. The only foundation that can be laid is Jesus Christ.

Each of us must build on this foundation and the quality of our work will be tested by fire - only the precious will survive 11-13.

3:16-23 **Temple of the Holy Spirit** We must understand that each believer is God's temple and the Holy Spirit lives in us v16. He is there to guide us in everything we do. Be sensitive to the voice of the Holy Spirit and learn to respond Gal 5:25. Also recognize that each believer is his dwelling which we should not offend. This will eliminate pride and boasting so that we can live with each other in humility, love and service - *all are yours and you are of Christ and Christ is of God v22.* **Live to receive praise from God**

4:1-21 **God will expose the motives of men's hearts** Then each will receive his praise from God. So we are answerable to God for our conduct and our actions. All we have we received – our life, our abilities, our salvation and our calling. We should humbly seek to outwork our service before God without boasting, complaint or fear of the opinion of others. We are fools for Christ, answerable to him, completely and only. *The kingdom of God is not a matter of talk but of power v20* - worked out through obedient lives as we apply the principles.

HIGH STANDARDS OF CONDUCT

5:1-5 **Immorality** – *the second issue.* There was sexual misconduct amongst the people. Such people who continue in these activities should be excluded from fellowship so they will realize the serious nature of their sin and repent.

5:6-8 Christ our Passover lamb has been sacrificed The death of Jesus on the cross was the fulfilment of the Passover sacrifice. When God delivered Israel from bondage in Egypt it was required that a lamb be sacrificed and the shed blood be sprinkled on the door to protect from death Ex 12:1-13. This was a shadow of the coming of Jesus. The Passover festival has been superseded by the Holy Communion. The shed blood of Jesus delivers us from the bondage of sin and death. As the Passover required bread without yeast (yeast representing sin) so the bread and wine of the Communion, a reminder of his life given for us, should be taken without guilty conscience over unconfessed sin, in sincerity and truth.

5:9-13 This does not mean we should not associate with people of the world. However people who profess to be believers but continue to live in unconfessed sin must be excluded from fellowship so that they might realize their error and repent.

6:1-8 Lawsuits against believers – *the third issue.* Believers could not come to agreement about disputes and were resorting to the civil law courts. This showed lack of trust and humility. If we can't apply the basic principles of our faith we are *completely defeated already.* It is a bad witness to the world so if we can't come to agreement it would be better to suffer wrong.

6:2,3 Future responsibility *Do you not know that the saints will judge the world? v2.* This is a deep truth and should produce in us a sense of humility, awe and commitment Rev 5:10. It should also foster the highest standard of personal conduct especially with regard to fellow believers.

6:9-11 *You were washed - sanctified - justified in the name of the Lord Jesus Christ and by the Spirit of our God v11.* When we accept Jesus as Savior we are cleansed – covered by his blood! The Holy Spirit then begins the work of sanctification, changing our inner being to conform to the image of Christ. As such we must turn away from the evil ways of the world. This is a continuing work of the Spirit with which we must be actively involved – put off the old, put on the new Eph 4:22-24; Col 3:1.

6:12-20 *Everything is permissible – but I will not be mastered by anything v12* Reverting to the problem of sexual immorality - a further point. While I have freedom in Christ yet my body belongs to him and must be treated as such. I am united with the Lord so I am one with him in spirit – my body is the temple of the Holy Spirit. So I must honor God with my body.

7:1-40 Marriage – *the fourth issue.* People were unsure about marriage due to the expected imminent return of the Lord v27. Marriage is honorable and requires commitment by both parties. Divorce should be avoided - it shows broken commitment with God Mal 2:15,16. A person who becomes a believer after marriage to a nonbeliever will have a sanctified family. Paul encouraged people to consider celibacy so they could give undivided devotion to God v35. Each person has his own gift in this regard v7. It is not a matter of outward show but *keeping God's commands is what counts v19.*

8:1-13 Food Sacrificed to Idols – *the fifth issue.* Worldly practices don't affect food. *Food does not bring us near to God v8.* However we should not offend others by the freedom we have in Christ. If something is a stumbling block to another person it is better for us to refrain for their sake.

9:1-23 The Rights of the Believer – *the sixth issue.* We all have rights – the ox should not be muzzled, the plowman should share in the harvest. *Those who preach the Gospel should receive their living from the Gospel v14.* But we should not demand that our rights be recognized. We serve because of our love for the Lord, not for personal recognition or reward v16. *I have become all things to all men so that by all means possible I might save some v22.* Our motivation should be the joy of sharing in the Gospel and its blessings.

9:24-27 The Christian life is comparable to a race We must run the race of life in such a way as to get the prize. That means strict training and discipline of the body. Our prize is a crown that will last forever. Many do not apply this principle.

10:1-10 Remaining True to the Faith – *the seventh issue.* The people of Israel who came out of Egypt under Moses did not keep the commands God had given them. Although they were God's chosen people and all received the initial blessing they turned away from God becoming involved in idolatry, immorality, testing the Lord, grumbling and other evils so that their bodies were scattered over the desert.

10:11 These things happened to them as examples and were written down as warnings for us, on whom the fulfilment of the ages has come. The Old Testament with all its instructions and history is important to us today. We learn from the experiences of the people as God dealt with them Lk 24:44.

As we read and meditate on God's Word we become acquainted with each of the characters – the righteous men made perfect Heb 12:23. They become our friends and they speak into our lives, for good and bad. We learn from them, from their successes and failures. We learn to apply the principles of faith and avoid the temptations of life Heb 11:1-40.

That is reason for daily reading of God's Word - so that we may learn from things that happened to the people in the past for we too are God's chosen people Rom 15:4.

10:12,13 Ability to Overcome We must be vigilant in our obedience and loyalty to the Lord, busy about his service. There is no room for complacency - it is so easy to fall into temptation. No test is new or too hard for us.

God is faithful; he will not let you be tempted beyond what you can bear – he will also provide a way out so that you can stand up under it v13. This is great encouragement that we can resist temptation, overcome opposition and achieve great things with the help that God has made available.

10:14-22 **Idolatry** – *the eighth issue.* We must not participate in demonic or godless activities. There are many practices that people adopt that demonstrate their hope in chance and the spirit world rather than placing faith in God alone.

When we take Holy Communion we share in the body and blood of Christ. Those who are involved in evil share with the devil, even if they do not admit it. You cannot have a part in both the Lord's table and the table of demons v21.

10:23-33 **The Freedom of the Believer** While we have freedom because of the death of Christ not everything is beneficial or constructive – for our own good or the good of others 6:12. We are not restricted in what we may eat but we should not offend the conscience of another. *So whether you eat or drink or whatever you do, do it all for the glory of God v31.* This is a guide for all our actions! Col 3:23,24.

11:1-16 **Conduct in worship** – *the ninth issue.* Guidelines for attendance at worship are given. While some of these points are cultural, worship should be conducted in a discreet, modest, respectful and reverent manner. Worship should be based on what people bring in thankful praise to God rather than what they expect to receive. The dependence on emotion and entertainment in worship at the expense of devotion, adoration and commitment weakens the believer Ps 63:1-8.

11:17-34 **The Holy Communion** – *the tenth issue.* Divisions over teaching and personalities were evident. They held a fellowship meal as well as sharing the Communion – a 'love feast' to celebrate their union in Christ. There was no concern for others – the wealthy overindulged, the poor went hungry. There was no order and especially no reverence for the Lord.

The sacred meaning of the Lord's Supper is given v23-26. This sacrament was requested by Jesus on the night he was betrayed Lk 22:19,20. We take it with thankfulness remembering that Jesus died for our sins 11:24,25; 1Pet 1:19. It is intended to be God-centered as a solemn occasion which must involve reverence and reflection, examining our lives to confess sin v28. To do it in an unworthy manner is a sin that brings judgment. This was the reason many were 'weak and sick' v27-30.

The Lord's Supper was celebrated regularly from house to house but particularly on the Lord's Day, the first day of the week, to commemorate the resurrection of the Lord Acts 2:46; 20:7; Rev 1:10. The new believers were quickly ostracized from the Jewish customs and were not required to keep them Acts 15:23-29.

SPIRITUAL GIFTS

12:1-3 **Spiritual Gifts** – *the eleventh issue.* There was much misunderstanding about the nature and purpose of the **Gifts of the Spirit.** Gifts occur because of the indwelling presence of the Holy Spirit within the believer and are given to edify the believers. It is necessary to test the source of a gift. Does a person testify that 'Jesus is Lord'? Is this evident in their conversation and life? Such a person will receive spiritual gifts.

The Seven-fold Ministry of the Holy Spirit was explained by Jesus Jn 14:15-17,25,26; 15:26,27; 16:7-15.

12:4-10 **Many manifestations** There are many different ways in which the Spirit works in the lives of individuals but all gifts, service and workings are because it is God who is working by his Spirit in each believer. To each born again believer an outworking (manifestation) of the Spirit is given for the common good of the body! The Spirit reveals himself in a practical way in each believer. Nine gifts are listed as examples – wisdom, knowledge, faith, healing, miraculous powers, prophecy, distinguishing spirits, speaking in tongues and interpretation of tongues. There are others Rom 12:4-8; Eph 4:11.

12:11 **The Spirit gives his gifts -** *to each person just as he determines.* It is the Spirit's choice and each believer must search this out in personal devotion.

12:12-31 **One body, many parts** All believers are part of the body of Christ, each with a unique function. This describes the intimate relationship which each believer enters into with Jesus and which is available to all believers.

God has arranged the parts in the body, every one of them, just as he wanted them to be v18. We each need the other and must respect the gifts of others – with no divisions.

Now you are the body of Christ and each one of you is a part of it v27. Each has a special role to play in ministering to the others. We should *eagerly desire the greater gifts v31* which minister to others in order for us to serve others better.

What are the ways the Holy Spirit has chosen to reveal himself through you for the benefits of others?

13:1-12 **The Royal Law of Love** - *the twelfth issue.* The people were interested in pursuing greater physical signs of their spirituality. It is the same in modern society – seeing is believing, otherwise it is not real! The primary indication of a changed Spirit-filled life will be the outworking of God's love in the heart and actions of the believer. All other signs recede into insignificance by comparison without it.

A description of love is given which is without peer. It first describes the nature and character of God, for God is love 1Jn 4:8. It then provides a pattern for the believer.

This love is contrasted with the love of human nature – family affection, friendship and physical romantic love.

This love of God is independent of the object or the response. God's love is based completely on the source and is unconditional Rom 5:8. It is poured out into our hearts by the Holy Spirit whom he has given us so that we may love like him Rom 5:5.

God's Love Defined -
• **Love is patient** – considerate, suffers long, when aspirations are not met Lk 15:20 - **I will love without demand**
• **Love is kind** – showing mercy as a deliberate response Lk 10:37 - **As a rose when crushed, yields up its perfume**
• **It does not envy** – no discontent, satisfied with what one has Phil 4:11,12 - **I choose contentment in all situations**
• **It does not boast** – no self-assertion, secure in one's personal position Gal 6:14 - **I will look for the good in others**
• **Love is not proud** – not self-centered – following the example of Jesus being the servant of others Mt 20:24-28; Eph 5:21 - **I will submit to others out of reverence for Christ**
• **Love is not rude** – always polite, considering the feelings and position of others - **I won't give offence**
• **Love is not self-seeking** – always considering others before self, especially family Rom 12:10; 2Cor 8:9 - **I will give myself to the welfare of others - without condition**

- **Love is not easily angered** – feelings under control, as an unprofitable servant Lk 17:10 - **I won't take offence**
- **Love keeps no record of wrongs** – responding as one forgiven Mt 6:14 - **I will not hold on to the burdens of the past**
- **Love does not delight in evil** – the ways and attitudes of the world Eph 2:1-3 - **I choose to focus on the greater things**
- **But rejoices with the truth** – seeking justice, righteousness and God's kingdom Mt 6:33 - **I will always pursue the truth**
- **Love always protects** – provides, defends, spares no effort Mt 7:9-12 - **I will honor my responsibility to those I love and serve**
- **Love always trusts** – develops an attitude of confidence and belief Phil 2;1-4 - **I will always be trustworthy**
- **Love always hopes** – looking for the good in all circumstances and people Rom 8:28 - **I will always expect great things**
- **Love always perseveres** – never giving up 2Cor 4:16-18 - **I will give my best even in the hard times**
- **Love never fails** – commitment for life Heb 12;1-3 - **I will never give up on the things I believe in.**

God's love is noted for the exceptions as much as for the inclusions - for what it is not as much as what it is!

It is good for us to have a regular personal performance appraisal using these qualities to consider the way we love others, our family and our colleagues – are we growing to be like Christ?

Such love cannot be fully appropriated without the indwelling presence and control of the Holy Spirit.

God's Love in Us We cannot apply this quality of God's love by personal effort. The wonder is that *God has poured out his love into our hearts by the Holy Spirit whom he has given us Rom 5:5.* So we learn to love others with God's love working in us. Mature faith gradually incorporates these qualities in the life of the believer as we are *transformed into his likeness with ever-increasing glory 2Cor 3:18.* Paul was inspired to present these aspects (qualities) of God's love in his letter about conduct as our guide for all actions towards others. The application of God's love will transform relationships in all areas of life

13:13 The key qualities of life are faith, hope and love – **but the greatest of these is love.**

14:1-25 **Prophecy and Tongues** There was a misuse of speaking in tongues (part of the eleventh issue 12:1). Tongues are for speaking with

God and for personal edification, unless someone interprets what is said. Prophesying is for strengthening, encouragement, comfort and edifying others and so is superior v5. It is good to pray with your spirit and also with your mind. But teaching is far more important than tongues v19. Tongues are a sign for unbelievers v22. It is essential that those who meet should understand what is being said.

14:26-40 **Order in Worship** - *the thirteenth issue.* Everything done in the meeting must be to strengthen the people. Praise, instruction in the Word of God, revelation, a tongue of interpretation, all are good – *be eager to prophecy and do not forbid speaking in tongues - but everything should be done in a fitting and orderly way v40.*

THE GOSPEL AND THE RESURRECTION
Having addressed the issues of concern Paul turned to the central focus of the Christian walk – to understand and proclaim the Gospel of Jesus Christ. All other concerns are secondary!

15:1-8 **The Gospel Defined –**
- *that Christ died for our sins according to the Scriptures*
- *that he was buried*
- *that he was raised on the third day according to the Scriptures.*

These three points are fundamental to Christian belief and are unique – other beliefs either deny or ignore this cornerstone of the Scriptures. The resurrection of Jesus is the one physical and historical fact that all people must come to a decision about – the answer determines one's eternal destiny. Whether this was a problem for the Corinthians Paul emphasized it again. It was the message he had received from the first disciples v1. The 'Scriptures' refer to the Old Testament! The resurrection of Jesus confirmed that he is the Messiah and the fulfilment of the prophets. After the resurrection Jesus appeared to the disciples and many others including Paul! v8. It is from Paul that we learn of the specific appearances to Peter and James v5,7.

15:9-11 **By the grace of God I am what I am** Paul's encounter with the risen Lord motivated his work Acts 9:5; 2Cor 12:2. But he saw himself as undeserving and so worked harder to please God – *his grace to me was not without effect. No, I worked harder than all of them - yet not I, but the grace of God that was with me v9,10;* Gal 1:13.

15:12-23 **Resurrection of the Dead** - *the fourteenth issue.* Because of the resurrection of Jesus we are confident that believers also will rise again as he promised Jn 6:40. The historical fact of the resurrection gives the assurance that all believers have because Christ is *the first-fruits of those who have fallen asleep v20.* Many are not prepared to look into the facts of the life, death and resurrection of Jesus because to do so would change their world view and lifestyle.

15:24-34 Then the end will come – after the resurrection of the saints Christ will reign over the kingdoms of the world. He will then hand over the universal kingdom to the Father once he has destroyed all dominion, authority and power Rev 12:10; 20:4. The resurrection of the believer is the promise of God and the basis for our commitment and hope!

15:35-41 **The Physical Body** Natural science is confined by definition to the physical world and so excludes the spiritual dimension. The fossil record is seen as progressive evolution of all existence from one elementary particle. There is no physical evidence of life after death except for the resurrection of Jesus. There is no purpose in live and no hope beyond the grave.

15:36-41 **A lesson from nature** A dormant seed does not come to life unless it dies in the ground! It becomes a new living entity – a flower, plant or tree. This is the pattern God has planned. There are many evidences of purpose in God's creation.

All flesh is not the same. God has given mankind one kind of flesh - animals, birds and fish other kinds v38,39. There are heavenly (spiritual) bodies and earthly bodies each with their own kind of splendor. The sun, moon and each star have their own splendor (how wonderfully true!).

15:42-49 **The New Spiritual Body** As there is a physical material world, there is a spiritual eternal world. When the physical order passes away, for the born again believer at the resurrection there will be a new spiritual body v42-44. Now sown as perishable it will be raised imperishable, now imperfect it will be glorious, now in weakness it will be powerful, now natural and physical it will be spiritual! v43,44.

God made Adam from the dust of the earth and a living soul (being) – the current state of each person Gen 2:7. The spirit of the natural person is dead to God. As a result of his sacrificial death Jesus is a life-giving spirit – he gives spiritual, eternal life to those who accept him as Savior and Lord Jn 1:12; 6:40.

What is more *so shall we bear the likeness of the man from heaven v49;* Phil 3:21; Col 3:4; 1Jn 3:2 – we will be like Jesus!

***15:50-53* Flesh and Blood cannot inherit the Kingdom of God** This statement removes all basis for hope for the unbeliever. However for the believer, just as we have been 'born again' to spiritual life through Christ, so our resurrection body will be spirit - not flesh, for flesh and blood cannot inherit the kingdom of God v50; Jn 3:5,6. We will be changed in an instant for the mortal must put on immortality v53. More details of the resurrection of the believer are provided in 1Thes 4:13-18.

***15:54-56* Assurance of Life after Death** This is the wonderful expectation of the believer. As a result of these great assurances death holds no fear for the believer - it is graduation from the training period of life to begin the real purpose of our eternal existence. To die is to be with the Lord in an instant Lk 23:43; 2Cor 5:8; Phil 1:23; Heb 12:23.

15:57,58 Thanks be to God! He gives us the victory through our Lord Jesus Christ. This is why we commit wholeheartedly to the work of the Lord *because our labor is not in vain! v58.*
This is the reason for our expectation and our endeavor.

***16:1-4* Collection of gifts for the poor** The believers (saints) in Jerusalem were in need due to famine under Claudius. They were also a minority in a capital city. Paul collected gifts from the Gentile believers which he would personally take to Jerusalem Rom 15:23-29; 2Cor 8:1-7; 9:1-5. This was a major reason for the planned return visit to Jerusalem Acts 24:17.

***16:5-24* Final Instructions** Be on your guard, stand firm in the faith, be people of courage, be strong, do everything in love v13.
Note the house church of Aquila and Priscilla v19

Evolution Issues 1Cor 15:31-41
We have the geological and fossil record which clearly shows structure in all matter. The concept of evolution has a logical base. However there are major problems with the theory of unaided development.
1. Natural science and biological evolution by random mutation and natural selection make no statement about the nature and purpose of God or mankind as they are confined by choice and definition to the physical world.
2. Evolution does not exclude the involvement of God who is Spirit. Many draw a conclusion that God is not required in order to understand the physical world because of the existence of physical laws and so

choose to ignore him. But they have no explanation for the origin of energy, existence or life. They also cannot explain the existence of the physical, biological and chemical laws.

3. The presence of the universe and human beings demands purpose and intelligence – the alternative is no purpose and no intelligence!

4. Evolution does not account for the existence of innate matter – the atom, electron, quark and the source of the initial energy.

5. Evolution cannot account for the occurrence of life from inert matter – the starting conditions & form of the first self-replicating systems are not known.

• the emergence of life from non-life – all evidence shows that only life produces life – was life inherent in the atom?

• the assumption of spontaneous generation which has never been detected or explained

• the emergence of order from disorder by natural processes – contrary to the law of entropy and all scientific investigation.

6. Evolution does not explain consciousness, intelligence and morality – the soul.

7. The moral order in the human being implies purpose, responsibility and accountability which exist in all cultures. Departure from moral order results in anarchy.

8. The fossil record identifies countless diverse forms of structure which are equally explained by purposeful, progressive design – as incorporated in all manmade inventions. One would expect that good features of lesser forms would be included in more complex models by an intelligent creator.

9. Evolution does not explain the mechanism that directs the process of natural selection from random, mindless disorder. Natural law does not cause, but only explains what happens.

10. Evolution denies the uniqueness of mankind as a moral being – responsible and accountable.

11. Evolution places the human being at the centre of one's personal world without accountability as a finite physical entity with no purpose and destined for extinction Ps 2:1-3.

12. Evolution and natural science make no contribution to the inevitable end of the process – the implication is oblivion – from nothing to nothing!

2 Corinthians

Introduction – During his third mission journey AD 54-57 while in Ephesus Paul received a letter and reports of bad conduct from Corinth. He responded with the first Epistle to the Corinthians 1Cor 7:1. It was delivered by Timothy. He likely also made a short visit to Corinth to reinforce the letter before returning to Ephesus 1Cor 4:19; 2Cor 13:1-3.

After leaving Ephesus he spent time in Troas and then moved to Macedonia where Titus came from Corinth with a positive report. This gave Paul great joy because the Corinthians had begun to correct their ways as he had instructed them 7:5-7, 13-16. He wrote this second letter because he still had not made a significant journey to Corinth as he had promised 13:10.

Paul then went to Greece for three months and then spent time (winter) in Corinth Acts 20:3; 1Cor 16:6. He had much to revise with them now that they had responded to his authority and teaching. This was his third visit to Corinth 13:1,2. There he likely wrote the Epistle to the Romans in preparation for his planned visit to Rome Rom 15:23-25; 16:23.

Author – Apostle Paul, from Macedonia to believers in Corinth.

Period – Around AD 56.

Theme – **Ministry of the Believer** The Corinthians began to reform their practices and conduct following Paul's previous letter. This teaching letter describes in detail the pattern of life for the believer. While presented in defense of Paul's apostleship it is a great personal guide to discipleship and encouragement to all who would live for and witness to Jesus Christ as Lord.

THE GOD OF ALL COMFORT

1:1,2 **The Believers are called Saints** – sanctified, set apart for God. The letter was intended for all believers throughout Achaia, the southern province of Greece.

1:3-10 **The God of all comfort** Praise is directed to the God and Father of our Lord Jesus Christ who is also the source of our comfort. Even as we suffer hardship and persecution for the name of Jesus we also receive comfort and encouragement. This equips us to comfort others. Our difficulties teach us to rely not on ourselves but on God. We are confident that as he has delivered us in the past he will continue to do so in the future.

1:11 Paul knew that our prayers are effective in the lives of others and in the work of the ministry.

All God's promises are confirmed in Christ.

1:12-20 Paul's plan to visit Corinth had been delayed. He assured them he was genuine, as all our commitments should be. We must always stand by our word.

All of God's promises have their fulfilment in Jesus v20.

1:21,22 **Our Guarantee - the Holy Spirit** God confirmed his promise of eternal life to us – *He anointed us, set his seal of ownership on us and put his Spirit in our hearts as a deposit guaranteeing what is to come.* This is the privilege, the experience and the assurance of all born again believers.

1:23,24 **By Faith You Stand Firm** In this materialistic, humanistic, pleasure seeking world the faith of the believer is continually on trial. It is by holding fast to the things we believe, as revealed in the Word of God and especially the promises of Jesus that we will triumph in the end Heb 3:6; 4:14; 10:23.

2:1-11 **Evil Schemes** One reason for the delayed visit was so that the Corinthians could have time to consider and implement the instructions in his previous letter(s). Having taken action against those who did wrong, if they have shown repentance they should now be shown forgiveness v7. Satan has schemes to use our differences and conflicts to outwit us causing disunity and ineffectiveness. We must be aware of them - always forgive and act in love – *do not give the devil a foothold Eph 4:27.*

MINISTERS OF THE NEW COVENANT

2:12-17 God always leads us in triumphal procession in Christ v14 – everywhere we go we can tell others about him. Having been saved from the penalty of sin and born again into new life we are able to testify to the One who saved us.

We are the fragrance of the knowledge of him - the aroma of Christ v14,15 – the smell of death to those who won't believe and the fragrance of life to those who are being saved.

3:1-6 **We do not need commendation from others** We are *a letter from Christ - written - with the Spirit of the living God - on tablets of human hearts v3.* God has made each of us ministers of the New Covenant.

3:7-11 **The Glory of the Covenants compared -**

- **The glory of the Old Covenant** was reflected in the face of Moses when he received the Ten Commandments on tablets from God. The Law brought condemnation and judgment and could not change lives - the physical glory faded away
- **The New Covenant** - the ministry of the Spirit is more glorious because it brings righteousness and transforms the lives of believers – the glory will continue for eternity v11.

3:12-18 **Being Made into God's Image!** Moses used a veil to shield the people from the reflected glory on his person.
But when anyone turns to the Lord the veil is taken away! v16. Now we can come to God in personal fellowship 'with unveiled face', nothing hidden or separating us from his Presence. As we commune with him through prayer and meditating on the Word of God we *are being transformed into his likeness with ever increasing glory through the Holy Spirit v18.* The hurt to God's image in us at Eden is being restored. We should expect to see this progressive transformation in each of our lives.

4:1-4 **The Desperate Need for the Gospel** We need to understand that *the god of this world has blinded the minds of unbelievers v4.* This emphasizes the importance of prayer and perseverance in our witnessing.

4:5-15 **Treasure in Jars of Clay** God has revealed the glory of the **Gospel of Jesus as Lord** to us weak individuals. We are like jars of clay, common vessels - yet containing great treasure. God has planned it this way so that the power of ministry will not come from us but will come from God v7. We have the message and we have an obligation to speak what we believe – that is how faith works v13,14; Rom 10:10.

4:16-18 **We Never Give Up** Outwardly we may suffer physically. Yet inwardly, spiritually we are renewed every day by fellowship with the Lord and his Word. We know the comparatively small difficulties we now *endure are achieving for us an eternal glory that far outweighs them all v17.* We focus on the things of the eternal kingdom – not of the world.

5:1-9 **Our Heavenly Dwelling** We have a new spiritual body after physical death that is kept by God and we long to enter that existence – when the mortal will be swallowed up by eternal life! All this has been planned by God and is confirmed by the Holy Spirit within us. We live by our faith, not by the physical world, looking forward to the time when we will dwell with the Lord. We aim to please God in everything because *we must all appear before the judgment seat of Christ* to give account.

5:10 The Judgment Seat of Christ While the eternal salvation of the believer is assured, there will be a time of recognition of the stewardship of each one when we come before the Lord Rom 14:10-12; 1Cor 3:9-15; 4:5. This was confirmed by Jesus in the parables he taught Mt 25:14-30; Lk 19:11-27.

Judgment of the Nations Those who have not accepted Jesus as Savior and Lord will also give account – they will be *judged according to what they had done as recorded in the books Rev 20:11-15.* This was also confirmed by Jesus in the parables Mt 13:41-43,49,50. This will be a fearful event when one considers the standard and the outcome Mt 5:48; 2Thes 1;8-10. It is motivation for our testimony to the unbeliever – *We implore you on Christ's behalf: Be reconciled to God 2Cor 5:20,21.*

THE MINISTRY OF RECONCILIATION

5:11-15 The Love of Christ Compels Us We want to tell everyone wherever possible about God's love, judgment and provision in Christ. *Christ's love compels us* – because of what he has done on the cross we should no longer live for ourselves but for him who died for us and rose again v14,15.

5:16-19 If anyone is in Christ he is a new creature – we have been reconciled to God (put right). So we no longer look at people from a worldly viewpoint but through the eyes of Jesus.

5:20 We are therefore Christ's ambassadors – we are his witnesses Acts 1:8. We speak to others on behalf of Christ, the King and urge them to be reunited with God.

5:21 God made Jesus to be sin for us What this means is a deep mystery. It shows both the gravity of the offense of sin and the enormity of the love of God for each person. The result is that we have the right to stand in the presence of God!

6:1 God's fellow workers It is incredible to think that we can change from being rebels to become partners with God. Yet that is what he has chosen to do – he gives us the privilege of working with him in leading other to him. This is one of the greatest moments for the believer – to be involved in seeing someone respond in faith to Jesus through the Holy Spirit.

In affirming his credentials and explaining his motivation for ministry Paul was always encouraging believers to understand that they had the same privilege and responsibility to proclaim the Gospel. He also took every opportunity to remind people of the urgency and necessity of making a commitment to Jesus.

6:2-11 Now is the Day of Salvation God's grace is available to all who will receive it. It is our task to tell people about salvation through Jesus. No effort should be spared, no trouble too great, no offence made – we need to speak freely and open wide our hearts to the unsaved.

6:14-18 We are the Temple of the Living God Paul recognized the indwelling presence of God through the Holy Spirit. So will every born again believer 1Cor 3:16,17; 6:19. We restrict our involvement with unbelievers as we do not want to be drawn to follow their ways Ps 1:1-6.

7:1 Perfecting Holiness We separate ourselves from everything that contaminates body and spirit pursuing holiness because of our reverence for God Heb 12:28,29.

7:2-7 The Personal Side of Paul – concern for the people - confidence, encouragement and joy in them. He also had inner fears in the conflicts he faced and was encouraged by fellowship and good reports. By faith he overcame them all 2Tim 4:7.

7:8-16 Sorrow before God over wrongdoing brings repentance and results in salvation with no regrets. This is compared with worldly sorrow that brings depression and death. Repentance also removes offense between people and encourages those involved, increasing the bond of affection.

8:1-15 Generosity God's grace causes us to give out of thankfulness for what he has given us! So we should give *as much as we are able and even beyond v3.* As we do our best in all areas of faith we should also excel in giving – this will test our sincerity v8. Our example is our Lord Jesus Christ – *though he was rich yet for your sakes he became poor so you through his poverty might become rich! v9.* We share so there may be equality amongst the believers v15. Paul collected gifts from the Gentile believers which he would personally take to Jerusalem Rom 15:23-29; 1Cor 16:1-4.

8:16-24 Administration It is important to have good administration of funds and resources through specially approved members and recorded procedures to avoid criticism and loss. Then people will be prepared to give more freely.

9:1-5 Paul found it necessary to actively encourage the grace of giving to the needy.

9:6-15 Grace is God's Indescribable Gift If we are not generous we receive little in return. Generosity comes back to us so - having all that you need, you will abound in every good work v8. *Freely you have received, freely give Mt 10:8.*

10:1-18 Credentials for Ministry Paul defended his apostolic ministry against criticism from competing teachers and deceivers. These guidelines apply for all people in ministry and especially our own. We do not use worldly attitudes and methods. Meekness and the gentleness of Christ are required. Then the **divine power behind our actions** breaks down every stubborn and proud mind that is against God so that people will come into obedience to Christ. This presupposes our own obedience to Christ v6. Our boasting should only be in the Lord because the one whom he commends is approved v18.

11:1-15 Conflict among leaders draws away from devotion to Christ. The devil masquerades as an angel of light. He uses pride, arrogance, disputes, inflated egos and false teaching to hinder the Lord's work v14.

11:16-33 Power Made Perfect in Weakness Paul set out his personal credentials which were significant – both in status and in service. He also described his suffering for the Gospel. But he preferred to boast about his weaknesses (not revealed – but could have been anything and refers to all our weaknesses) v30.

12:1-10 He even experienced visions v2. However the Lord taught him that *my grace is sufficient for you, for my power is made perfect in weakness v9* – we should accept our weakness recognizing that Christ's power will be revealed in us. Our best effort is as 'loaves and fishes' yielded to him Mt 14:17,18.

12:11-21 The Sign of a True Minister Real concern was expressed for the spiritual and moral condition of the Corinthians. The conduct outlined in v20 was clearly contrary to the standard of believers in Christ. As Christ is in us we will see his influence in our thoughts, attitudes and conduct.

13:1-13 Aim for perfection *v9* Though we are weak, we live in God's power. This is our goal - as he is perfect! Mt 5:48.

THE TRIUNE GOD

13:14 The Christian God is Triune This is the main distinction between the one true God and the man-made gods of the world. This unique truth comes from revelation alone. The Scriptures explain that

God is One and that he is revealed as three distinct Persons. We primarily encounter the Trinity as –
- **Father** – the Creator who sustains all things by the Word of his power and has a perfect plan for each person
- **Son** – the Savior who laid aside his glory in order to died for the sins of the world and rose again as Lord
- **Holy Spirit** – the indwelling presence of God in the heart of the believer to guide and empower in the work of ministry.

We need to worship and engage the Triune God in this way.
Paul gave a clear indication of the primary functions of the Trinity in relation to man -
- we encounter God's love through the Father
- we experience God's grace through the Son our Lord Jesus Christ and
- we appropriate God's fellowship and guidance through the Holy Spirit!

Only those who have been born again into the spiritual realm of God can comprehend and appropriate this wonderful truth Jn 1:12,13; 3:5-7; 4:23,24.

Understanding the Trinity
While revealed throughout Scripture, the most detailed understanding of the Trinity was presented by Jesus. He spoke of my Father Jn 14:13 – your heavenly Father Mt 6:26; 7:11 – our Father Mt 6:9.
He clearly identified the relationship between the Father and the Son Jn 10:30 – the 'only begotten of the Father' Jn 1:14,18; 3:16. He confirmed the coming and the work of the Holy Spirit – 'proceeding from the Father and the Son' Jn 14:26; 15:26.
A number of physical examples have been suggested to explain the Trinity. Care must be taken in approaching the nature and Persons of the Godhead. We must be entirely guided by the Scriptures in profound awe and anticipation.
Benefit can be gained by reference to the Creeds (Apostles, Nicene, Athanasian and Chalcedon Creeds).

Galatians

Introduction – Paul spent most of the time on his first mission journey with Barnabas in the Roman Province of Galatia in southern Asia Minor where they started churches at Pisidian Antioch, Iconium, Lystra and Derbe. After they left, Judaisers came from Jerusalem to Galatia telling the believers that they had to obey Jewish laws and customs as well as believing in Jesus in order to be saved. Paul received information about this problem in the home church at Antioch, Syria where similar claims were being made. He wrote this teaching letter to the Galatians to refute these demands. This matter became a major issue as many Jewish people responded to the Gospel. However many remained supportive of the Pharisees and retained Jewish customs. Many Jews acted antagonistically to the Gospel.

The issue was soon resolved for the Christian church by the apostles at the Jerusalem Council Acts 15:1-21.

Author – Paul told the story of his personal ministry journey in first person giving a good indication of his teaching and lifestyle for comparison with other letters which bear his name.

Period – This is the earliest of Paul's letters and was written from Antioch, Syria around AD 49 (less than 20 years after the Ascension). It was before the great Council in Jerusalem and before his second mission journey. It is possibly the earliest apostolic document available.

Theme - Freedom from the Law through faith in Jesus Christ alone
As a result of the perfect life and sacrifice of Jesus the sins of the believer are forgiven and the indwelling presence of the Holy Spirit provides the ability to serve God.

Paul also defended his authority and teaching as a result of those who denounced him.

SUMMARY
Credentials of an Apostle 1:1-24
Defense of the Gospel 2:1-21
Justification by Faith in Christ Alone 3:1 to 4:31
Freedom in Christ Through the Holy Spirit 5:1-21
The Fruit of the Spirit 5:22-24
Outworking of the Freedom 6:1-18

CREDENTIALS OF AN APOSTLE - *called by God!*

***1:1,2* The Gospel Declared** Jesus Christ gave himself for our sins, according to the will of God the Father who raised him from the dead in confirmation of his acceptance of this act! Rom 1:2-4. This is verifiable historical fact.

***1:3-5* The Lord Jesus Christ** Just as the first address of Peter gives full emphasis to the authority of Jesus as Lord and Christ (the Messiah, Anointed One) so Paul recognized the Lordship of Jesus from his conversion Acts 2:36; 9:5. He too was convinced that Jesus had been exalted to the highest place by God. This title became the focus of his ministry. In the last day *at the name of Jesus, every knee should bow, in heaven and on earth and under the earth, and every tongue confess that Jesus Christ is Lord, to the glory of God the Father Phil 2:10,11.*

***1:6* The Problem** Some Judaizers (those who wished to enforce Jewish customs on the new Gentile believers) came to Antioch in Syria from Judea. They wanted to compel Gentile believers to observe Jewish laws and rituals, particularly the act of circumcision. While this was considered compulsory by the Jews it was not essential for salvation as a result of the sacrificial death of Jesus. Paul also received word that the believers in the province of Galatia where he and Barnabas had ministered were being undermined by these Jews who were adding to the Gospel. He wrote the letter to the Galatians at this time in defense of his authority and teaching Acts 15:1,2. He challenged them about the foolishness of their compromise.

***1:7-10* Only One Gospel** The 'other or different gospels' required acceptance of laws and deeds and are not founded on the sufficiency of faith in Christ alone. Such beliefs have no power to change people or to ensure life after death.

Paul had already given the Lord Jesus Christ equal position with God the Father indicating the deity of Jesus v3. He confirmed that the death of Jesus has the power to free from sins and guarantees eternal life to the believer v4 - this is the only Gospel.

***1:11-24* Paul's Calling and Preparation** Paul declared that he was an apostle appointed directly by Jesus through his Damascus vision v1; Acts 9:4-6,15,16. He also professed his conviction that Jesus was raised from the dead both because he had seen him in a vision and now experienced him in his daily life v12.

Paul had an experience of Jesus, both when he was confronted on the way to Damascus Acts 26:15 and also possibly during his time in Arabia v17; 2Cor 12:3. This explains his dedication to the Gospel. He was a zealous Jew who persecuted the church till he was converted to become a follower of Jesus v13. He came to see himself as having been the chief among sinners 1Tim 1:15.

After his conversion Paul spent time in Damascus and a period of meditation in Arabia (three years) v17. He made a visit to Jerusalem where he was not generally accepted through fear of his past persecution before returning to his home city of Tarsus Acts 9:19-30. He was recruited from there by Barnabas to assist in teaching and discipling the large number of Gentiles at Antioch who were new in the faith 1:21; Acts 11:25.

DEFENSE OF THE GOSPEL
Sufficiency of Christ alone for salvation

2:1-10 **The Visit to Jerusalem** Fourteen years after Paul's conversion Barnabas and Paul (Saul) went to Jerusalem with a gift from the Antioch church Acts 11:30. There they had private discussions on the *freedom we have in Christ Jesus* without the need for Jewish customs v4. Paul emphasized to the Galatians that the leaders in Jerusalem, James, Peter and John agreed with the message Paul and Barnabas were preaching and gave them full authority to preach to the Gentiles v9.

Not long after this Barnabas and Paul went on their first Mission Journey to Galatia Acts 11:1-4. On their return the dispute over Jewish customs arose both in Antioch and Galatia.

2:11-14 **Peter in Antioch** About this time Peter visited Antioch. At first he mixed freely with Gentiles but withdrew when Jews from Jerusalem arrived v11. Paul challenged Peter for this inconsistency v14.

Apostolic Declaration This matter was resolved at a major Council in Jerusalem in AD 50 Acts 15:1-21. Paul and Barnabas went to Jerusalem and reached agreement with the leaders that Jewish customs were not required for salvation as it was based on the sufficiency of the death of Christ alone. This was supported by the evidence of the power of their ministry in Galatia. It was also agreed that Paul and Barnabas continue to work with the Gentiles (non Jews) Acts 15:1-35. This was an important event because it confirms the basis of the Gospel.

2:15-19 **Faith in Jesus Christ** Paul presented this detailed explanation in his letter to the believers in Galatia so that they could see the

47

importance of being justified by faith in Jesus Christ without the need to observe the law.

2:20,21 *I have been crucified with Christ – Christ lives in me – I live by faith in the Son of God* This is Paul's brilliant summary of his faith in Jesus Christ as the only and all-sufficient means of salvation. It also encourages our commitment to make Jesus the central focus of our daily life. This is in contrast to the need to follow a burdensome set of laws and rituals Acts 15:10.

It took a devout Pharisee to realize the full implication of the work of Jesus on the cross.

JUSTIFICATION BY FAITH IN CHRIST ALONE

3:1-14 *Who has bewitched you* Having confirmed that the apostles in Jerusalem had accepted the Gentiles by faith Paul challenged the Galatians for turning back to Jewish customs. They had come to believe in Jesus and seen miracles at Paul's hand. They had also received the experience of the Holy Spirit in their lives. This was due to faith, not by following customs.

Abraham is our example as he *believed God and it was credited to him as righteousness* (right standing with God) v6. He was accepted by God because of his faith, without the law. Those who rely on observing the law must meet all the requirements of the law at all times – they are under a curse if they fail in only one point of the law v10; Deu 27:26.

3:13,14 *Christ redeemed us from the curse of the law by becoming a curse for us!* This is the amazing truth of the Gospel. The curse of the law is the penalty of death. Because of sin we are condemned to separation from God for eternity. By his death on the cross Jesus paid the penalty, removed the offense and delivered the believer from the curse of death. The one who has faith in Jesus Christ takes part in *the blessing given to Abraham – by faith we might receive the promise of the Spirit v14.* We have been delivered from all curses and are now under the blessing of God Gen 12:2,3; Num 23:19,20.

3:15 to 4:7 God's promises still apply The promises God made to Abraham were to his 'seed' (singular) – the Seed is Christ! The Jewish law given to Moses on Mt Sinai did not set aside God's promises given previously to Abraham. The law was given to guide people to be aware of sin and to allow sin to be forgiven through the substitutionary sacrifice of an animal until the Seed should come. Now that Christ has come we are no longer under the supervision of the law but we receive the promise of God through Christ alone 3:22-25.

Through faith in Christ Jesus and his redeeming death on the cross, the following promises apply to all who believe -
* you are all sons of God through faith in Christ Jesus 3:26
* you are all one in Christ Jesus, with every believer 3:28
* you are redeemed and have the full rights of sons 4:4
* you have the Spirit of God's Son in your heart, who leads you to address God as Father! 4:6
* you are no longer a slave but a son of God and because of this God has made you an heir with Christ 4:7.

4:8-31 Further reason for faith Before acknowledging Jesus as Savior and Lord the Galatians had to follow the principles of past beliefs. They were under the basic principles of the world – which include having no relationship with God and seeing death without hope of eternal life v3,8. When they came to faith in Christ they were set free from these things and from the burden of having to follow the law. Now Paul had to start all over again to bring them to faith in Christ alone v19.

They were special to Paul as his first significant outreach.

He used the comparison of the two sons born to Abraham – Ishmael born to Hagar the slave woman and Isaac born to the free woman Sarah. Hagar represented the Old Covenant which was given on Mt Zion and referred to the physical Jerusalem.

Sarah represented the New Covenant based on the spiritual Mt Zion and the heavenly Jerusalem Heb 12:22. By faith in Christ we are children of the New Covenant – free of the law v26.

FREEDOM IN CHRIST THROUGH THE HOLY SPIRIT

5:1-12 For freedom Christ has set us free Because Christ died for us we no longer have to observe outward rituals or depend on our own efforts in obeying the law in order to be in right standing with God – *the only thing that counts is faith expressing itself in love* v6. This great truth was introduced by Jesus – *if you hold to my teaching you are really my disciples – then you will know the truth and the truth will set you free* Jn 8:31,32. This freedom is a wonderful, liberating daily experience for those who are born again Mt 6:25-34; 11:28-30.

5:13-15 Do not use your freedom to indulge in the sinful nature v13. Relationship with God through Christ sets us free from the power of sin and death and allows us to serve God freely. But we know God is holy and we must not abuse this freedom. Rather than being bound by laws and religious observances we are to live for God and show our faith by the way we live our lives – in following the example of Jesus.

The entire law is summed up in a single command: 'Love your neighbor as yourself' v14; Mt 22:37-40; Jn 13:34,35. Rather than laws of constraint God's love in us expressed to others will maintain blessed unity.

5:16-18 *Live by the Spirit* This is the means by which we live the Christian life and resist temptation to sin. The sinful nature is still active in us and is in conflict with what the Spirit wants. Rather than responding to the sinful nature we are able to respond to the indwelling presence of the Holy Spirit who transforms us from within. *If you are led by the Spirit, you are not under the law v18.*

5:19-21 Human Nature The actions of the sinful nature are described. These traits are evident to varying degrees in the lives of all people and believers must turn from them. No doubt Paul recognized that these issues were evident in the lives of the Galatians and warned them of the consequences v21.

THE FRUIT OF THE SPIRIT

5:22-24 The Nature and Character of God When a person is born again the Holy Spirit creates a new nature in the believer. This is the beginning of sanctification. We are sanctified before God because of the righteousness of Jesus. The work of sanctification in us continues as the Holy Spirit transforms us to be like Jesus. He produces the 'fruit of the Spirit' in us.

Some aspects of this fruit are *love, joy, peace, patience, kindness, goodness, faithfulness, gentleness and self-control v22.* The last of the fruit on this list is 'self-control'. This really means bring oneself under the control of the Holy Spirit. It is only by the power of the Spirit operating within that these qualities can develop fully in our lives.

Notice there is only one 'fruit' – it develops in our lives as we fellowship with the Holy Spirit, read God's Word and grow in our love for Jesus. There are many aspects of the fruit which represent the nature and character of God. Further aspects include faith, hope, forgiveness, repentance and integrity Mt 5:1-16; Rom 15:13; Jas 3:17,18. Jesus set the goal - *be perfect, therefore, as your heavenly Father is perfect Mt 5:48.*

The fruit will be recognized both personally and by others as it appears in our lives. Jesus said *by their fruit you will recognize them Mt 7:15-20.*

5:25,26 Since we live by the Spirit let us keep in step with the Spirit v25 As Jesus on earth walked with the disciples throughout their daily lives they hung on every word he spoke. In the same way each believer now has the Holy Spirit dwelling in them to guide, comfort and empower them.

Our aim is to be sensitive to the leading of the Holy Spirit who will guide us in everything we do. He not only tells us how to act and what to do he gives us the power to do it. Especially he will empower us to tell others about Jesus Jn 14:16,25,16; Acts 1:8.

OUTWORKING OF THE FREEDOM

6:1-13 Some practical matters of conduct -

• Temptation is ever present. We need the support of regular fellowship with other strong believers – and they need us! v2

• Pride is a constant test - we must each walk humbly before God looking to him for recognition v3

• We are to be generous in all things – sowing to please the Spirit v6 - remember that we reap what we sow

• Do not become weary in service or in doing good to others.

6:14-18 May I never boast except in the cross of our Lord Jesus Christ v14. Because we are a new creation, born again of the Spirit, this will impact every aspect of our life and everything we do. If we focus on Jesus and follow his example we will demonstrate that we are a new creation by the way we walk, talk and live 6:15.

Ephesians

Introduction Three doctrinal letters were written by Paul while under house arrest in Rome -
- Ephesians – Our position in Christ
- Philippians – Joy in Christ
- Colossians – The Supremacy of Christ

Ephesus was a major city on the west coast of Asia Minor and on the main east west trade route. It was first visited briefly by Paul at the end of his second mission journey on the way back to Jerusalem AD 53 Acts 18:19,20. He returned on his third journey AD 56 Acts 19:1-41 and spent several years establishing a church. It was a particularly idolatrous city but became a main center for the church in Asia.

Author – Paul wrote this letter around AD 60.

Period – During the two years Paul was under house arrest in Rome waiting to be tried before Caesar on charges laid by the Jews in Jerusalem Acts 28:30. It was possibly a circular letter to other churches in Asia as there are no specific issues raised Col 4:16. It was delivered by Tychicus 6:21.

Theme – Our position in Christ Jesus In prison after twelve years of teaching and mission endeavor all of Paul's revelation of God's plan was brought together in this letter. It consists of a general outline of Christian doctrine describing the purpose of God for the creation and in human history – the mystery of Christ! It gives the most detailed explanation of the spiritual world into which we are born again.

'In Christ Jesus' - this is the blessed state of being as a consequence of all that Jesus has done for us and what we have become because of his work. Understanding what it means to be 'In Christ Jesus' is a key priority of victorious living.

The Armor of God - there is a battle for the souls of mankind. In order to stand we need to apply the *'whole armor of God'*.

If we know that we are –
- **seated** with Christ in the heavenly realms and
- **walking** with the Spirit in the new way of life - then we will
- **stand** effectively against the devil and live a victorious life.

SUMMARY
God's Plan for You 1:1-23
New Life in the Heavenly Realms 2:1-10
Jesus is our Peace 2:11 to 3:21
A New Society 4:1-16
New Standards 4:17 to 5:20
New Relationships 5:21 to 6:9
The Christian Conflict 6:10-24

GOD'S PLAN FOR YOU – Life 'In Christ Jesus'

1:1,2 **Saint** – one who is set apart, not by personal merit but by selection, for a special purpose – to be holy. A saint is also 'faithful' – having faith in Jesus and exercising faith in daily life. To identify some as saints more than others is to detract from the need for every believer to demonstrate their individual sainthood. To pray to saints is to detract from the One who calls us to pray to the Father who hears us in the name of his Son Jesus Christ Jn 14:13,14; 15:16; 16:23-26.

Life 'in Christ Jesus' - God has provided all we need to live victorious and effective lives as we experience our relationship with Jesus through the Holy Spirit.

1:3 **We live in the Heavenly Realms** We are encouraged to live in an attitude of continual praise and thanksgiving to God. Why? Because we have been brought into a state of continual spiritual blessedness as we live our lives 'in Christ Jesus'. We find cause for thanksgiving in every situation because of who we are and what God has done for us 1Thes 5:16-19. The heavenly realm is the location where we experience all of these blessings.

The Heavenly Places or Realms – There is a physical, material world and a spiritual, heavenly world. The physical world is temporary while the heavenly world is eternal – the dwelling place of God. The physical being must be 'born again' into the spiritual world in order to live eternally with God 1:12,13; 2:1,5,6; 3:5-7; 4:23,24. As we have learned by practice to live in the physical world we must also learn by practice to live in the spiritual world.

The heavenly world is the dimension where we experience fellowship with God - Father, Son and Holy Spirit – where we walk in the Spirit every day 5:18-20.

The heavenly world is where we exercise our faith – where we set our hearts and minds on the things above Col 3:1-3. It is the unseen spiritual world, beyond the physical senses where discipleship is lived out – through thoughts, decisions, attitudes, temptations, commitments, faith, trust, hope and victory. We must base our understanding on what the Bible says.

The heavenly realms are -
- where we have every spiritual blessing in Christ 1:3
- where Christ is raised and seated at God's right hand 1:20
- where we have been made alive with Christ 2:5
- where we are raised with Christ and seated with him 2:6
- where our spiritual conflict takes place 6:12
- where angels, authorities and powers, all things are in submission to Christ 1Pet 3:22
- where the devil has been disarmed by the cross Col 2:14,15.

1:4-8 **Our Position 'in Christ Jesus'** We have been -
- **chosen by God** before the creation of the world to be blameless in his sight – this is a mystery v9
- **predestined** – our destiny was determined and assured by God before we were born v5
- **adopted** – spiritual rebirth brings us into the status of 'child of God' by his grace – his free unmerited favour v5
- **redeemed** – taken from bondage to the world and placed in God's kingdom – the price paid in full v7; 1Pet 1:18-21.
- **forgiven** – the offence of our sin removed by the shed blood of Jesus – the penalty of sin borne by Jesus v7.

This was all in accordance with God's pleasure and will v9.

1:9-12 **The Mystery of His Will** The purpose of the creation, previously hidden, has now been made known to us – it is to bring all things in heaven and on earth together under Christ when human history has run its course.

From the beginning of civilization all empires, kingdoms, nations and authorities have aspired to create the perfect system so that man can live in justice, peace and prosperity – every state has eventually failed through corruption, nepotism, self-interest, weakness or moral degradation. These aspirations will be fulfilled in the coming kingdom of God as he works out everything in conformity with the purpose of his will.

1:13,14 The Seal of the Holy Spirit The Holy Spirit brings conviction of sin, repentance, new birth and sanctification. He lives within the believer and his presence is the guarantee that we are God's possession.

1:15-23 Prayer for Growing Spiritual Understanding
Every believer must develop continually in three areas -
• we need to grow in our knowledge of God – *so that you may know him better v17* - we do this as we receive God's wisdom and revelation daily through the indwelling Holy Spirit
• we need to understand *the hope to which he has called you* both in this life and eternity - *the riches of his glorious inheritance in the saints v18* – we do this as our hearts are flooded with light
• we need to know and experience the working of God's *incomparably great power for us* - to keep us secure in our faith, to ensure our eternal future and to provide all we need to be effective witnesses v19; Acts 1:8. It is the same power that raised Christ from death and seated him at God's right hand where he reigns over all things both now and in eternity v20. He is now far above all rule and authority, power and dominion in the heavenly realms v21; Rom 8:37-39.
He is head of the church and all things are under his feet v22.
As the head of the body he fills each member so that they may become the full expression of Jesus to the world in the same way as he is the full expression of God to us v23; Col 1:18,19.

NEW LIFE IN THE HEAVENLY REALMS
2:1-10 What God has done for us in Christ Jesus
• Once we were dead to God because of sin v1 - we were under the power and influence of Satan and the ways of this world following our own desires and thoughts – this is the current condition of the natural person v3 – as explained by Jesus Jn 5:24-26
• He made us alive with Christ – we were born again v5
• We are no longer under the control of the ruler of this world, the spirit that is now at work in those who are disobedient v1-3
• He raised us up and seated us with Christ v6
• He plans to express his incomparable grace and kindness to us in eternity forever v7 - *the riches of his glorious inheritance in the saints! 1:18.*

2:8,9 We are saved by grace alone All this is because of God's grace, not because of anything we have done.

2:10 We are his workmanship God created us, prepared us and put each one of us in our present location with special work already arranged for us to undertake. He has redeemed us and brought us to this point in time so that we might fulfil our preordained purpose in extending his kingdom v10.

We need to KNOW these things –
- who we are in Christ Jesus – based on what God has already done for us as a result of the finished work of Jesus 1:4-14
- where we are in Christ Jesus – *raised us up with Christ and seated us with him in the heavenly realms* where he has all authority – and above our every circumstance 2:6
- what we are in Christ Jesus – righteous, we have "right standing" with the Father Phil 3:9 – God's workmanship 2:10
- what we have in Christ Jesus – every spiritual blessing 1:3
- what we can do in Christ Jesus – we are no longer under the ruler of this world – you no longer have to sin 2:1-3.

To know – means to see or understand as fact – to have fixed in the mind and memory – ultimately to be able to apply!

JESUS IS OUR PEACE

2:11-18 The Death of Hostilities We were separated from God as a result of our sinful human nature and subsequent actions - we were excluded from the covenants of the promise and without God in the world v12. But now we are brought into relationship with God through the blood of Christ v13. He became our peace – our means of achieving peace with God v14.

- He destroyed the barrier that stood between us and God
- He removed the dividing wall of hostility
- He abolished in his flesh the law with its commandments and regulations which held us captive due to inability to fulfil them.

His purpose was to create in himself one new man v15- uniting Jew and Gentile (for we were all in the same condition) - and in this united body to reconcile both of them to God through the cross. By this means *he put to death their (our) hostility v16.*

Through him we both have access to the Father by one Spirit v18 – both Jew and Gentile, all people who respond!

That they may be one If the death of Jesus on the cross brought believers peace with God and peace with fellow believers by destroying that dividing wall of hostility, how dare we again build hostility between ourselves and other believers! Jesus prayed *Holy Father, protect them by the power of your name – so that they may be one as we are one Jn 17:11.* The divisions within the Church today and within denominations are responsible for much of the ineffectiveness of believers and the poor image of the Church in the eyes of the unbeliever. We need to put aside differences and return to the common unified Gospel message of salvation through faith in Jesus Christ alone Jn 3:16; Mt 28:18-20.

Jesus prayed that we might be one as he is one with the Father - brought into complete unity that the world may know that the Father sent him Jn 17:20-26. It is good and pleasant to God when we work in unity - for there he bestows his blessing Ps 133:1-3. The world is desperate for this unified message. May the Lord make us willing to cooperate - to work together in unity!

2:19-22 Members of God's Household We are united with believers of all nations and can come to the Father by the Holy Spirit. Those who accept Jesus as Savior and Lord become fellow citizens of heaven and members of God's own household – a holy Temple in which God chooses to live by his Spirit v22. We are the body of Christ! v15; 4:4,15,16.

3:1-13 We may approach God This is the mystery of Christ – that through him all believers become heirs of God's family, members of one body and sharers in the promise of eternal life. Paul became a servant of this message to make known to all *the unsearchable riches of Christ v8.*

Every believer has this privilege to make this message known to all, as well as to the rulers and authorities in the heavenly realms - this has been God's eternal purpose and was accomplished for us in Christ Jesus our Lord v12.

Approaching God in freedom and confidence v12 Having been forgiven our sins through the death of Jesus we may now commune with the Father at any time Heb 10:19. This was a great comfort to Paul and is now the privilege of every believer v13. This relationship should be part of our daily walk.

3:14-19 Growing Spiritual Relationship with Christ We now can acknowledge God as **Father**! He is the One from whom every father and family in heaven and earth derives their name.

We need to grow in this relationship

Paul defined this prayer which applies for all believers -

- to be strengthened with power by his Spirit in our inner being v16 – this develops as we step out in faith each day
- so that Christ dwells (resides) in our hearts through faith v17; Col 3:15-17 – as we respond daily to the spiritual disciplines
- being rooted and grounded in love, to comprehend and to know God's all surpassing love more fully v17,18.

Then we will be filled completely with the fullness of God.

3:20,21 Do you know –
- He is able to do way beyond all we ask or imagine (immeasurably more!)
- His power is at work within us
- to him be glory in the church and in Christ Jesus!

A NEW SOCIETY – The Body of Christ

The Church is the 'body of Christ' This describes the intimacy of our relationship with Christ and also with all other believers! So we must live lives worthy of God – to which he has called us - being completely humble, gentle and patient exercising love to each other and making every effort to keep the unity that the Holy Spirit brings! Because we have been united with all believers we are encouraged to be like Christ in our relationship with every other believer Phil 2:5-11. We have a common message to proclaim – Jesus saves! Here is the definition of the ideal church and believer!

4:1-3 The Character of the Believer Living a life worthy of the calling you have received -
- **completely humble** - the absence of pride, preferring others
- **gentle** – not meek, but strength under control – all abilities and gifting in the hands of Jesus Mt 11:29
- **patient** - persevering in tribulation and prayer, never giving up on people or the task
- **bearing with one another** - longsuffering, tolerant, working for the good of another - to seek the highest good of others
- **love** - God is love, self-giving love, who fills the believer and overflows from us to others Rom 5:5; 1Cor 13:1-13
- **unity** - striving to maintain the relationship Christ has won for us with common focus on the task of extending the kingdom – the Holy Spirit brings this unity, why do we break it?
- **peace** - pursuing harmony with God and others Eph 2:14-18.

***4:4-6* The Faith of the Believer** As we are each part of a unified body we hold to a unified core belief –

• **one body** - believers are all members of the body of Christ who is the head of the church - each has a unique part to play as decided by God 1Cor 12:27

• **one Spirit** - the Holy Spirit fills each believer and brings unity to the whole body which we are called to maintain

• **one hope** - the guarantee of salvation and eternal life through faith in Christ alone

• **one Lord** - Jesus is Savior and Lord over all, the only name under heaven given to men by which we must be saved Acts 4:12 – believers die for this belief

• **one faith** - believing that Jesus saves from sin, sickness and evil, through faith alone and we are called to make this known

• **one baptism** - baptism signifies forgiveness of sin and rising to a new life - the outward sign of inner spiritual rebirth

• **one God and Father of all** - there is one God who is revealed as triune in nature – Father, Son and Holy Spirit.

***4:7-13* The Ministry of the Believer** Every member has a ministry and is given the necessary ability to perform it -

Ministry Gifts - Jesus has given gifts to each member. First there are the 'ministry gifts' of apostles, prophets, evangelists, pastors and teachers v11. These gifts are given to church leaders for the purpose of preparing God's people for works of service - to equip the saints for the work of ministry v12.

Other gifts are listed including the 'service gifts' Rom 12:6-8 and the 'spiritual gifts' 1Cor 12:7-11.

***4:14-15* Body Ministry** As each member is equipped for the work of the ministry and released to use their specific gifts, under the leading of the Holy Spirit, the whole body grows to complete unity, knowledge and maturity in relationship with Jesus in full measure v13.

***4:16* The Body Builds Itself Up** When equipped in this way we will no longer be led astray by every false teaching and opinion. Instead the body will build itself up in love, as each member works effectively.

NEW STANDARDS

***4:17-32* Put on the New Person** As members of the body -

• we put off the old way of life in the futility of thinking

59

- we put on the new way in the attitude of our minds having our focus based on righteousness and holiness v24; Mt 7:13,14.

Truth and love replace falsehood and bitterness. We do not grieve or cause offense to the Holy Spirit v30.

5:1-20 **Imitating God** As we grow in our relationship with the Lord his nature and character replaces our previous practice of conforming to the ways and standards of the world. Light replaces darkness - we are children of light. Then we will be continually filled with the Holy Spirit v18. Our conversation will be filled with songs and words of joy and encouragement to one another v19. We will continually be expressing praise and thanksgiving to God the Father and Jesus our Lord v20. This is the pattern of life for the believer.

NEW RELATIONSHIPS

5:21 **Submit to one another out of reverence for Christ** – This is the principle that will transform every relationship – to respond to each person as we would to Jesus. All relational problems dissolve when we take on this attitude.

5:22-33 **Family** Wives and husbands have love and respect for each other based on the love that Christ has for the church (this is a profound mystery) v32. Men particularly come to recognise the responsibility before God for their wives and for protection, provision and upbringing of their children Mal 2:13-16.

6:1-4 **Mutual Respect** Children and parents respond in mutual regard and cooperation.

6:5-9 **Workplace** A new respect applies in the workplace - servant leader and worker Mt 20:25-28. Commitment comes through motivation – recognition comes through commitment.

6:7 **We are really serving the Lord** Service and relationship is possible when we undertake every action and response based on this fact. When we come to the point where we can see Jesus in each person and realise that we are his representative our attitude changes from one of self-centeredness to service Col 3:23,24. This attitude grows in us as the Word of Christ dwells in us richly Col 3:17-22.

THE CHRISTIAN CONFLICT - The Armour of God

6:10-24 Finally be strong in the Lord and in his mighty power - When a person is born again they have entered a new relationship with

God and so come into greater conflict with the devil in the battleground of good and evil. Once we have embraced and are appropriating the knowledge of the first five chapters we are able to face this conflict. We cannot stand in our own strength but *in the Lord and in his mighty power v10.*

We do not fight against people (flesh and blood) other believers or unsaved.

But we do struggle, wrestle, contest - with the rulers, authorities, powers of this dark world and against spiritual forces of evil in the heavenly realms who would destroy our faith or make us ineffective v12. This struggle is the daily experience of the Christian – otherwise we are already defeated and in submission (prisoners)!

We are called to stand against these evil forces, to hold our faith and to be effective in advancing God's kingdom.

God has provided armour for protection, defence and attack so we can hold our position v13.

There are seven pieces of armor and we may see seven major areas of attack -

• **Belt of Truth** – the devil wants us to believe this is our world and here for our enjoyment. **Fact** - We must embrace the truth in God's Word that this is God's world and we have a duty to believe in him, to live by his ways and to tell others about him v14; Mt 28:18-20; Col 1:28,29

• **Breastplate of Righteousness** – the devil tells us we are not good enough or that we do not need forgiveness. **Fact** - God's Word tells us that we have the righteousness of Jesus by faith and are acceptable to God v14; Rom 1:17; 3:22; 2Cor 5:21

• **Boots of the Gospel** – the devil tells us we don't have the knowledge or ability to save others. **Fact** - God's Word says we must prepare ourselves so we can be equipped and ready to tell others about Jesus and the plan of salvation at any time v15; 2Tim 2:15; 1Pet 3:15

• **Shield of Faith** – we are attacked by doubts like flaming arrows about who we are in Christ and what God is asking us to do. **Fact** - We stand on Scripture ground by declaring that God's Word is true and that it works effectively in our lives v16. **God said it, I believe it, that settles it** Rom 10:17.

Of course to do this we need to know God's Word and be growing in knowledge by regular reading if we are to use the shield of faith.

61

- **Helmet of Salvation** – we sometimes doubt if we are really born again. This is the knock-out blow. **Fact** - We must believe God's Word that we are born again because we have accepted Jesus as our Savior v17; 1Jn 5:11,12
- **Sword of the Spirit** – we begin to think that reading God's Word is not important to our daily life. **Fact** - The Word of God is the only weapon of attack – we may hold our faith with the other pieces of armour but will be ineffective and discouraged without growing in the knowledge of the Word of God. The way to victorious living is by taking the Sword of the Sprit – God's Word, and reading it, memorizing it and meditating on it daily v17; Heb 4:12,13; Mt 4:1-11. In this way we can 'rightly handle' the Word of truth.
- **Prayer in the Spirit** – we will be discouraged from praying. **Fact** - We must learn the habit of praying 'in the Spirit' on all occasions, with all kinds of prayer, with all persistence, for all the saints. We should pray for missionaries, church leaders and fellow believers – those who are in less prosperous situations than us v19; 1Thes 5:16-19. We should pray regularly for national leaders and situations around the world 1Tim 2:1-4.

Prayer is the method of engagement The armour is not just for our own personal use but to make us effective in serving in the kingdom. Our activities and plans should be begun, continued and ended in prayer.

Vigilance – Having learned of the dynamic nature of the church at Ephesus in AD 60 we find that within thirty years despite their zeal and perseverance they had lost their first love Rev 2:4,5. This serves to reinforce the importance of vigilance in applying the spiritual disciplines outlined in this letter.

In Christ Jesus I Am - Ephesians 1:1-14

It is faith-building to repeat aloud each promise after saying 'In Christ Jesus I am ....'

- a Saint – a faithful believer 1:2
- thankful – praising God for everything 1:3
- blessed – with every spiritual blessing in the heavenly realms 1:3
- chosen – to be holy and blameless in His sight 1:4
- predestined – in love before the creation of the world 1:5
- adopted – as His sons by His pleasure and will 1:5
- accepted – freely – to the praise of His glorious grace 1:6
- redeemed – through His blood, reconciled with God 1:7
- forgiven – of my sins and justified before God 1:7
- enlightened – with wisdom and understanding 1:8,9
- given an inheritance – according to God's eternal plan 1:11
- sealed – with the Holy Spirit as a guarantee of eternal life 1:13
- assured – that I am God's possession 1:14
- raised and seated with Christ in the heavenly realm 2:6
- to receive the incomparable riches of God's grace forever 2:7
- continually being filled with the Spirit 5:18
- a child of Abraham Rom 4:16
- a king and I reign in life Rom 8:17
- a super conqueror Rom 8:37
- God's child who is born again by the Word of God Rom 8:16
- an heir of God and a co-heir with Christ Rom 8:17
- filled with all joy and peace as I believe in Him Rom 8:29
- abounding in hope by the power of the Holy Spirit Rom 15:13
- being transformed into the likeness of Christ 2 Cor 3:18
- a new creation 2 Cor 5:17
- rescued from the present evil age Gal 1:4
- crucified with Christ Gal 2:20
- a citizen of heaven Phil 3:20
- eagerly waiting for the Lord to return Phil 3:20
- rejoicing in the Lord always Phil 4:4
- able to do all things through Christ who strengthens me Phil 4:13
- giving thanks in every situation 1 Thes 5:17

Awareness of this special relationship 'in Christ Jesus' was first noted in Colin Urquhart, In Christ Jesus, Hodder & Stoughton, London,1981.

Philippians

Introduction – Philippians is one of the three doctrinal letters written by Paul while under house arrest in Rome. Philippi lay 13 km from the south east coast of Macedonia named after Philip II father of Alexander the Great. Paul visited in AD 52 on his second mission journey Acts 16:12. This was the first of the churches he established in Europe which opened the way into Greece. He returned again in AD 55 Acts 20:1-6.

Author – The apostle Paul wrote this letter around AD 60.

Period – During the two years Paul was in Rome waiting to be tried before Caesar on charges laid by the Jews in Jerusalem Acts 28:30. It was possibly a circular letter to other churches in Asia as there are no specific issues raised Col 4:16.

Theme – Joy in Christ In prison after years of teaching and missionary endeavor Paul described the joy of living a Christ-centered life. Victorious living comes through a personal abiding relationship with Jesus. This relationship impacts every part of life and brings real and lasting joy Jn 15:11 -

- it is lasting, ever present joy, that no one and no circumstance can take away from us Jn 16:22,24
- it is the full measure of the joy of Jesus within us Jn 17:13
- it is joy that is inexpressible and glorious 1Pet 1:8
- joy is also one of the fruit of the Spirit Gal 5:22.

JOY IN PRAYING

1:1-11 **The Saints** – all who are in relationship with Jesus. We are each sanctified, set apart for God's service.

We are encouraged to pray frequently knowing that our prayers are important to God. Prayer produces joy that God puts in our hearts as we continue to pray v4. The lack of joy in prayer should motivate us to pursue our relationship with the Lord.

We can be confident that the work begun in us will be carried on to completion when Christ returns v6.

Prayer for others shows our love for them. This is what we should pray for them v9-11 -

- that their love may abound in knowledge and depth of insight
- that they may discern what is best in every action v10 and
- that they may grow in 'Christ likeness'.

We are also called to pray for leaders and government and for the salvation of all people 1Tim 2:1-8.

We should pray and never give up! Lk 18:1-8.

Lack of prayer and joy in prayer shows doubt in the effectiveness of prayer. There is much misunderstanding about prayer which tends to discourage us instead of it becoming a joy.

JOY IN PROCLAIMING CHRIST

1:12-30 **For Me to Live is Christ and to Die is Gain** Paul was in prison because the religious leaders in Jerusalem wanted to stop the spread of the Gospel. However more people were now talking about Christ and this made him glad. Our aim should be in all things, even in conflict, persecution and difficulties that Christ be exalted in us v20. He looked forward to the joy of life after death but he also saw this life as the opportunity to lead others to Christ and strengthen them in their faith v25,26. This is also our opportunity. As we pursue the joy of serving we look forward to the joy to come Ps 126:5,6. We must stand together in one spirit as one body to proclaim the Gospel even if it involves suffering v29.

JOY IN BECOMING LIKE CHRIST

2:1-4 **Becoming like Christ** Evidence of being born again will be like-minded unity in our efforts to serve Jesus with humility, without pride, conceit or self-centeredness and living for the interest of others.

2:5-8 **The attitude of Christ** We have the example of Christ to follow in unity, humility and service.

We also see the incarnation of Jesus as truly God and Man -

• He was in very nature God v6 – as Son of God, Jesus possessed eternal pre-existence with the Father Jn 1:1-4,14,16-18; Col 1:15-17; Heb 1:1-3

• He did not grasp at his position of equality within the Godhead – in contrast to the pride and self-seeking of mankind

• He chose to lay aside his position of greatness

• He emptied himself - made himself nothing – of no reputation – it was the Father's will and the Savior's choice v7

• He took the nature of a servant – to do the will of the Father

• He was made in human likeness – born of woman that he could take on our humanity and the burden of our sins

• Being found in appearance as a man – he became truly human, except without sin v8

- He humbled himself and became obedient – the duty of mankind is to worship, obey and serve the Creator God
- even to the point of death on the cross – it was a criminal's death – for one who had no fault – for those who deserved to die.

In the example set by Jesus we see the mystery and wonder of the salvation of mankind and the pattern we should follow. No effort is too great when we consider what Christ has done for us.

Jesus is Lord As a result of the obedience of Jesus God exalted him to the highest place and gave him the name that is above every name. The time will come when every person will bow the knee and every tongue will confess that *Jesus is Lord to the glory of God the Father v6-11.* The deep significance of this recognition relates to the fact that God is declared as Lord, king and judge Is 33:22; 43:15; 44:6; 45:23.

2:12-18 **Shining Stars – our sanctification** We are sanctified in God's sight by the work of Jesus on the cross. There are two further aspects of sanctification – how we are being made holy by the indwelling presence of the Holy Spirit -
- the first is from our side – we are required to work at our faith with diligence, awe and reverence for God. We do not earn favour but we give our best effort in response to all that God has done for us in Christ Jesus
- the second part is provided by God through the Holy Spirit – he works in us to give us the will and ability to do what he wants as we respond to the leading of the Spirit.

We work in partnership with him! v12,13. The result is that we will be more like Christ every day. As we follow the leading and the example of Jesus we will shine like stars in the universe being an example for others to follow and attracting people to Jesus Mt 5:16. This will bring inner gladness as we rejoice in the Lord v18. The joy comes as we are refined to be more like him.

So if we are still on earth we know it is for a purpose - God has work to do either through us, or on us!

2:19-30 **Two Examples** Timothy and Epaphroditus were also good examples of shining stars. The worldly attitude requires everyone to look out for their own interests. These two did not look out for their own interests but for the interests of Christ v21. Epaphroditus had come from Philippi to Rome with a gift for Paul and became sick. He was now being sent back well again.

JOY IN KNOWING CHRIST

3:1-11 **Rejoice in the Lord** There is real and lasting joy in knowing Christ. It is sometimes spontaneous and at other times must be sought. The key to victorious living is to focus on our relationship with Jesus, not on the circumstances that surround us. Of course we must deal with the daily situations by thought and planning. But if our joy is in worldly success alone we will be frustrated. Real joy only comes from the Lord – the joy of Jesus in us Jn 15:11. *The joy of the Lord is your strength Neh 8:10.* We live and worship by the Spirit of God and put no confidence in worldly recognition or reward v3. All things come second to our love for him v7. We have righteousness that comes from God by faith in Christ v9.

We need to actively grow in our relationship with Christ with the power of His resurrection outworking in our lives v10.

3:12-21 **Press On to the Goal** We are called to press on towards the goal and the prize of eternal life v12. Our future is with Him – we are citizens, not of earth but of heaven. When he returns he *will transform our lowly bodies so that they will be like his glorious body v21.*

JOY IN THE PRESENCE OF CHRIST

4:1-9 **There are six practical steps to growing in the joy of the Lord**. As we have learned to relate so well to the physical world through a lifetime of practice, so we must learn by practice to apply the principles of living in the spiritual world into which we have been born again -

• **Praise** v4 The need to rejoice in the Lord always is emphasized as the first step 3:1. Praise is the normal response to a relationship with the Almighty and the atmosphere in which the Holy Spirit operates. Praise and thanksgiving should continually be on our lips Ps 63:3-5. Such joy is only possible as we learn to focus on the Lord – in every situation 1Thes 5:16–19

• **Platform** v5 That the Lord is near reminds us of the indwelling presence of the Holy Spirit and the need to stand on the platform of Scripture ground. We need to know and apply what Christ has gained for us in the heavenly realms – who we are in Christ, based on what he has done for us – where we are in Christ, raised and seated with him in the heavenly realms – what we are in Christ, we have "right standing" with the Father – what we have in Christ, every spiritual blessing in the heavenly realms and what we can do in Christ, no longer under the ruler of this world, we no longer have to sin! Eph 1:3 to 2:1-3. This is the platform on which we must stand – base our confidence

• **Presence** v6 In his presence we are freed from anxiety about anything as we learn to commune with the Father Heb 10:19-22. In everything we can pray, petition, give thanks and make our requests known to him. As we learn to continue to live in him we will overflow with thankfulness Col 2:6,7. David knew this joy that comes from walking in God's presence Ps 16:11

• **Peace** v7 As a result of developing our relationship with him the peace of Christ comes on us and it guards our heart and our mind. This is a peace which is independent of circumstances, beyond human understanding and that the world can't take away – it rules in our hearts Col 3:15. We are protected and guarded from the attack of the enemy's fiery darts of doubt Is 26:3,4

• **Perspective** v8 We begin to see things from God's perspective. Instead of being under the circumstances we rise to our place in the heavenly realms where we are seated with Christ. Our attitude changes to a positive outlook, walking, talking, thinking 'kingdom conduct' Col 3:1. Our focus changes from worldly things to things of the Spirit Rom 8:5-8. We receive his guidance, becoming 'controlled' by the Holy Spirit Rom 8:9-12. We receive the heart of the Father with self-giving love for fellow believers, love for the unsaved, a burden for the lost and a desire to be involved in mission.

Joshua and Caleb saw the Promised Land through the perspective of God's promise – not through the inadequacies of the people Num 13:26-30; 14:6-9. David saw the giant through the eyes of his relationship with God – not through the fear of the army 1Sam 17:1-58.

• **Practice** v9 We are encouraged to work at these things and to put them into practice. We need to 'practice the presence of Jesus'. We learn to acclaim him – to walk in the light of his presence - to rejoice in his name all day long and to exult in right standing with him! Ps 89:15-17.

JOY IN CONTENTMENT

4:10-12 **The Secret of Contentment** As we grow in our relationship with Jesus our focus changes from our own interests to the work of the Lord. We recognize that our own resources are complemented by the provision of the Lord. We find that there is contentment that comes in any and every situation v12. We realize that God is sovereign in all things and that he cares for us. He knows our needs and he has our situation in his hand - this is the walk of faith Mt 6:25-34. He works with us to complete his plan for our lives and has guaranteed us eternal life 1:6. He will also ensure that we achieve the tasks he has called us to.

As we develop our trust in him we discover the secret of contentment v12. This secret must be learned by practicing the spiritual disciplines of prayer, reading the Word, worship, fellowship and witnessing Acts 2:42-47.

In considering our own circumstances remember that on the first visit to Philippi Paul and Silas were stripped, severely beaten and put in prison in stocks. Their praise resulted in God's action and salvation for the jailor's family – they were filled with joy Acts 16:22-34. Paul learned to turn persecution into praise, hardship into results, circumstances into contentment! 2Cor 11:23-29

4-13-23 **Confidence in the Lord** Walking with the Lord develops confidence in our ability to be led into new situations that will extend our faith and bring glory to God.

• We learn that we can do all things through Christ who gives us strength to carry out everything he lays on our hearts v13.

• We also discover that God will supply all we need according to his glorious riches in Christ Jesus v19 – *'if you can?' said Jesus. 'Everything is possible for him who believes' Mk 9:23.*
This also requires practice Pro 3:1-12.

Colossians

Introduction – Colossians is one of three doctrinal letters written by Paul.

Colossae was among a group of small cities in central Asia Minor including Laodicea and Hierapolis where churches were established 4:13. It was some 150 km east of Ephesus where Paul spent several years on his third mission journey AD 56 Acts 19:1-41. While a visit by Paul to Colossae is not mentioned 2:1 the church was attended by his coworker and fellow servant Epaphras who may have founded it. He came to visit Paul in Rome 1:7. Paul planned to visit Colossae in anticipation of his release Phm 1:22.

Author – The apostle Paul wrote this letter around AD 60.

Period – During the two years under house arrest in Rome Paul wrote to Colossae Acts 28:30. It was intended as a circular letter to other churches in Asia 4:16.

Theme – The Supremacy of Christ in all things
- the pre-eminence of Christ before the creation of all things
- the supremacy of Christ in his work of revealing God and bringing about salvation for mankind
- the supremacy of Christ in the life and work of the believer.

THE SUPREME TRANSFORMATION

1:1,2 **The saints** are holy and faithful – they include all those who share in the kingdom of the Son he loves v2,4,12,13,26.

1:3-8 **The importance of prayer** While prayer, though often neglected, is important for our daily needs and the needs of the nations prayer with thanksgiving is also emphasized. We need to give thanks continually for the blessings we receive.

The people were motivated by hope and love in the Spirit v8.

1:9-12 **Spiritual growth** Paul prayed continually that the believers would go on in their new life to be filled with the knowledge of God and his will so that they would live worthy lives pleasing to the Lord v9. As we grow in our knowledge of God we will *be strengthened with all power according to his glorious might v11.* Then we will be patient in bearing fruit as we joyfully give thanks for our inheritance in the kingdom of light v12. It is this knowledge of God and his power that the believer needs to know in the individual life today.

1:13,14 The Kingdom of the Son This is the wonder of the Gospel! We who were alienated from God and were his enemies, have now been rescued out of the power, authority and control of Satan. We have been translated into the kingdom of the Son he loves. This translation is present tense and occurs in the life and experience of the believer. A cosmic change took place when Jesus died on the cross.

Redemption - our sins which separated us from God are forgiven, the penalty has been paid by Jesus and we have been reconciled to God - we have eternal life 1Jn 5:11,12.

This eternal kingdom was announced by Jesus Mt 4:17; 13:43, foreseen by the prophets Is 9:7 and will be fulfilled at the second coming of Jesus Rev: 11:15; 12:10.

THE SUPREME CHRIST

1:15-24 The one who has made this transformation in us possible is Jesus Christ the Son of God -

- He is the image of the invisible God v15 - God is Spirit and in Jesus we see the nature and character of God clearly revealed on earth in physical form Ex 33:19; Jn 4:23,24
- He will rule over all things as King of kings and Lord of lords v16; Phil 2:9-11; Rev 19:16
- All things that exist were created by him and for him v16
- He is before all things and in him all things hold together v17
- He is the head of the body, the church v18
- He is the beginning of the new kingdom and the first of many to rise from death v18; Rev 1:5
- In all things he has the supremacy v18; Rev 19:16
- All the fullness of God dwells in him v19.

By the blood of Jesus which was shed on the cross God made it possible for those who have faith in him to be reconciled to God v20. We were separated from God by the offense of our sins. Now we are made holy in God's sight, without blemish and free from accusation v22.

The supreme issue No other person in history can compare with Jesus. No other philosophy or belief has such a promise of forgiveness and eternal life. We ignore or reject him and his offer of salvation at our peril. To continue in faith the believer needs to be established and firm, immovable in the truth of the Gospel v23,24; 2:7.

THE SUPREME TASK

***1:24-27* Christ in You, the Hope of Glory** The mystery is that God could remove the offense of sin by the death of his Son so that Christ could dwell in the heart of the believer. This indwelling presence produces the assurance of sharing the glory of Christ in eternity. This mystery foreshadowed by the prophets is now revealed to include the Gentiles so we are without excuse if we deny it Is 2:2-4.

***1:28,29* We Proclaim Him - Declaring Christ is a matter of attitude** It is the joyful task of every believer to tell everyone about this truth -
- we warn those who don't believe - about the need to respond to Jesus – we are his ambassadors, evangelists Acts 1:8
- we teach those who do know so they may grow - we minister our gifts so that they may become more like Christ

We do this so that we may present everyone **perfect in Christ** – this is our aim!

This means we have an obligation to everyone we meet. God provides his energy that works so powerfully in us to carry out this task if we are responsive v29.

Perfect in Christ - the process of sanctification in the life of the believer continues daily as we are made more like Jesus 2:6,7; 2Cor 3:18,19. This takes place as we live **'in Christ'** – developing our relationship with him Eph 1:4-8.

Disciple Makers In order to be prepared to participate in this task we need to equip ourselves to -
- grow continually in our knowledge of God and the Scriptures
- know the Plan of Salvation and how to lead an enquirer through it using the Bible Rom 3:21-31 (ref p7)
- know how to lead someone to the point of accepting Christ
- be able to present a brief testimony of how we came to accept Jesus - what I was like, how I came to accept Jesus, what life is like now (in three minutes)
- prayerfully ask 'Lord, lead me to someone today!'

***2:1-5* Firm in the faith** There are many 'fine-sounding' arguments that distract people from the essentials of faith. This is the reason for being vigilant in growing in our relationship with Christ and our understanding of the mystery of God.

***2:6-12* Living with Jesus as Lord** Growth in the life of the believer is essential and ongoing so they may become encouraged in heart and united in love - with the full riches of understanding about Christ in their lives v2.

Receiving Jesus as Savior The way to enter into this mystery is to receive Jesus as Savior, acknowledge your sins, earnestly repent and ask him to come into your heart Jn 1:12,13. He has promised that he will come in Rev 3:20. This is the moment of being born again through the Holy Spirit – you have eternal life.

Receiving Jesus as Lord This is only the beginning! Having received Jesus as Savior you must recognize that he is the Lord! You need to continue to live in him v6 by applying the spiritual disciplines of growth, to become rooted and built up in him, strengthened, established in the faith as the Word of God teaches 1:23. Then you will overflow with thankfulness v7.

Depending on Jesus We must not be influenced by worldly traditions or human logic v8. This is a problem in all generations – faith in our own opinions and reasoning rather than in God's Word. Just as righteousness comes from God by faith, from first to last Rom 1:17 so life in Jesus requires depending on him from first to last living each day by faith in him!

This is not a matter of philosophy, human wisdom or opinions of the world.

The Divine Nature We have seen that all the fullness of the Deity lives in bodily form in Christ 1:19. Now **we have the divine nature in us** because we are 'in Christ' v9,10. This takes place when we are born again Jn 1:12,13. Jesus now lives in us and supplies the power and ability for us to put off the old sinful nature. Baptism symbolizes the death and washing away of the old nature and the rising of the new nature made alive in Christ v12. Jesus explained this relationship like a vine and branches – *apart from me you can do nothing Jn 15:5.* We must draw from him and stay connected.

THE SUPREME DEFEAT

2:13 **Set free from sin** We were spiritually dead because of our sins and our sinful nature. The nonbeliever does not realize that this is the condition of all who ignore God Eph 2:1-3.

2:14,15 **God made us alive with Christ** God's holiness and righteousness requires that the law be fulfilled and so we carried a debt as a result of our sin – a debt we could not repay. But the death of Christ in our place took away the debt – it was cancelled and nailed to the cross. This is the meaning of **atonement** – the offense of our sin was removed from before God. The mercy of God has obliterated the certificate of debt that was against us. That which hindered our fellowship with God no longer exists when we are included in the redeeming work of Christ Acts 3:19.

The powers and authorities that were against us were disarmed, defeated - their hold over us was broken – this was the triumph of the cross that set us free from the penalty and power of sin and death Mic 7:19.

2:16-23 Freedom found in Christ We are no longer tied to legalism, outward show and false humility. We are set free from man-made customs. The early Gentile believers were pressured to adopt Jewish customs. There was a range of spiritual and philosophical beliefs. Many challenged the deity of Jesus. Religious ordinances and rules were a shadow of things to come, a pattern of the reality which we now have received in Christ v17. We have died with Christ to the principles of the world and so are no longer under their influence v20. Faith is not shown in outward observances but in the conduct of our lives v23.

THE SUPREME LIFE

3:1-17 Raised with Christ We can live a new victorious life. As Christ is the center of our salvation so we focus our life on him by setting our hearts and our minds on things above – the heavenly realms, where Christ is seated at the right hand of God. This is the dimension to which we have been raised in the spirit Eph 2:6. While we live in the physical world we recognize the reality of the spiritual world in all situations and the abiding presence of Jesus through the indwelling Holy Spirit.

When Christ, who is the center of our life appears we also will appear with him in glory v4; 1Cor 15:49; Phil 3:21.

As we focus on Christ we put to death the old ways v5-9 – we don't focus on them anymore. It is like taking off old clothes and putting on new – adopting a whole new perspective. The direction of our focus determines our thoughts, our interests and ultimately our actions and commitment Rom 12:1,2. As we do this we are being renewed by knowledge in the image of God v10.

Victorious living is dependent on our relationship with Christ who *is all and is in all v11.*

A list of godly qualities is given - compassion, kindness, humility, gentleness, patience, forgiveness of others. These are all part of the fruit of the Spirit which we expect to see developing in our lives. Over all and in all is love - God's love in us, which binds all things together in perfect unity v12-14.

3:15 **The Peace of Christ** As we apply these principles – walking with Christ as Lord, the peace of Christ rules in our hearts - it takes over our anxieties and binds us together.

3:16,17 **The Word of Christ** That is why we need to read the Word of God daily – *let the Word of Christ dwell in you richly v16;* Jn 15:7 – as we live and meditate on God's Word we encourage one another and overflow with thanksgiving and joy. We live victorious lives and are a blessing to others v15 doing everything for the Lord Jesus, knowing that we are really serving him, giving thanks to God through him v17,23; 1Cor 10:31; Eph 6:7; Col 3:32. Our actions are based on the joy we will have when we meet the Lord! v14.

3:18-25 **Specific Conduct** The born again believer will have a new attitude toward all people, family, work and service Eph 5:21 to 6:9. They will apply themselves to everything they do with all their hearts and effort *as working for the Lord* v17.

4:1 **Masters** Leaders are responsible to God for the way they motivate and maximize the potential of each individual. Their success depends on the performance of the ones the direct.

4:2-18 **Coordination of the Churches** Paul worked hard to focus the believers to pray for one another and for outreach v1-4. He sent his coworkers to the centers for communication and encouragement v7-9. There were few Jewish people working with him v11. There were many home groups v15. He instructed the churches to circulate their letters v16.

4:10,14 **Mark and Luke** were together with Paul and had ample opportunity to research their Gospel accounts.

4:12,13 **Prayer** Epaphras as a key member of the church was *always wrestling in prayer* for the believers - a reason for their success.

1 Thessalonians

Introduction – Thessalonica was the capital city of Macedonia where Paul started the church on his second mission journey. After Paul and Silas were released from prison in Philippi they moved with Timothy south west to Thessalonica where Paul taught in the synagogue for some three weeks Acts 16:40; 17:1. A number of Jews and many Gentiles including women believed. But they were forced to leave quickly due to persecution from Jews envious at loosing synagogue members. Timothy returned to Thessalonica and subsequently brought a good report to Paul in Corinth of progress with the believers in Macedonia 3:6.

Author – The apostle Paul writing from Corinth around AD 51.

Period – An early letter with basic doctrine and encouragement.

Theme – Holiness in living because Jesus will soon return.

A MODEL FOR SERVICE

1:1 **In God the Father and the Lord Jesus Christ** This greeting expresses the unity of the Father and the Son Phil 2:5,6; Col 1:15. That the church is 'in the Father and the Son' describes the blessed relationship of salvation - brought about by the Father through the sacrifice of the Son Col 1:19,20.

1:1-3 **A Strong Young Church** Paul emphasized the need for prayer for all the believers. The result was work produced by faith, effort prompted by love and endurance inspired by hope in expectation of the return of Jesus. Pray that these qualities develop in all our groups.

1:4-10 **Preaching of the Gospel** was accompanied by power, evidence of the Holy Spirit and deep conviction in the people – further confirmation of fervent prayer. As a result the people wanted to follow the example of Paul and of Jesus - this produced joy in them given by the Holy Spirit.

The Return of Jesus Commitment and perseverance develop as we live, looking forward to the return of Jesus v10. This was central in the teaching of the early church and needs to be the focus of the believer today Jn 14:1-3.

A MODEL FOR MINISTRY

2:1-12 **Sharing the Gospel** often brings strong opposition. Our motives for serving are questioned. We should not look for recognition, praise or gain but faithfully tell what we know - we are answerable to

God. As followers of Christ we are to care like a mother towards those God brings across our path giving oneself as well as the message v7. We are also to act like a father to them – encouraging, comforting and urging worthy living v11. We should work to support ourselves and not be a burden on those we serve.

2:13 The Word of God The disciples knew that the message they spoke about Jesus as the Messiah was the Word of God and a further revelation to the Old Testament. Paul was encouraged when the people received it as such and he saw the Word working in them - as it should in us v13.

The Word of God actually does work in you who believe We must always base our life, faith and message on the Bible understanding that it is the source of power in teaching, preaching and growing. The Word of God is God-breathed and works in the life of the believer as it is applied 2Tim 3:16. It is also the source of the victorious life – as bread is to the body so the Word is to the spiritual life of the believer Mt 4:4; Deu 8:3.

2:14-16 Persecution Those who seek the truth will always find resistance from those who don't want change Mt 5:11,12; Eph 6:12,13; 2Tim 3:12. We see here confirmation of the intense persecution of the believers by the Jews which drove them out of Jerusalem even referring to the crucifixion Acts 8:1.

2:17,18 There are many things we can't do due to circumstances, priorities and restraints.

2:19,20 Our Glory and Joy is the knowledge of those we have seen come to the Lord. One of the great joys is to see the Holy Spirit at work in the life of one who we seek to bring to the Lord - it is holy ground.

3:1-5 Follow Up When a person responds to Jesus as Savior it is vital to follow them up as soon as possible to help them understand what has actually happened – that they have been born again. We must introduce them to prayer and the Word and arrange to spend time with them so they will be equipped to grow. We need to share our relationship with Jesus with them. Otherwise the devil will move in with doubts v5.

3:6-10 An Encouraging Report It is a joy to hear a good report that people are standing firm in the Lord – that joy is also shared in the presence of God! v8,9. Evidence of growth is when we see *love increase and overflow for each other and for everyone*. This is in answer to our prayer night and day v10,12.

3:11-13 **Father and Son at Work** The unity of the Godhead is again recognized in our plans, prayers, strengthening and expectation of the coming of the Lord Jesus Jn 5:17.

4:1-12 **Living in order to please God** As we grow in the Christian life we should expect to become stronger in all areas of commitment and belief. This is the ongoing developing process of sanctification – being made holy, which is brought about by the presence and work of the Holy Spirit in our lives. It means progressively being made more like Christ 2Cor 3:16-18.

Immorality was a way of life and is a sign of moral deterioration in society v3. We must learn to control our body to bring honor to God. Pure love for one another demonstrates God's love working through us and should increase as we mature in our faith v9. Our way of life should lead to self-sufficiency and respect of others v11.

THE COMING OF THE LORD

4:13-18 **Life After Death** There is much ignorance about death! For the believer death is like falling asleep – not a time of grief like those without hope but a time of great expectation.

Paul had taught that Jesus will return soon 1:10; 4:16; 5:1,2.

Just as Jesus died and rose again so those who have put their hope in him will rise again and never die v14; Jn 11:25,26 -

- the Lord will come down from heaven v16
- the dead in Christ will rise first v16
- those who are alive will be caught up together to meet him v17
- we will be with the Lord forever v17

This is just as Jesus promised Mt 24:31; Jn 14:1-3. It is also as John saw in the vision of the harvest of the earth Rev 14:14-16; 1Cor 15:50.

This knowledge is great encouragement for those who believe – compared with those who have no hope or expectation of life after death v13,18.

5:1-3 **The Day of the Lord** will come like a thief in the night, suddenly and unexpectedly. It will involve all who have accepted Jesus Christ as Savior and Lord. People will be living normal lives – two in the field, one will be taken, one will be left Mt 24:36-43. Those who are left face another fate.

*5:4-9 **You are all children of the light*** We know to expect this and will not be caught by surprise. We live lives that are ready for the return of Jesus – self-controlled, strong in faith, love and hope.

5:10,11 *He died for us so that - we may live together with him*
Because Jesus died to pay the penalty for our sins we know we have
eternal life – we will live together with him, forever - this was confirmed
by his resurrection from the dead. So whether asleep or alive we live in
his presence.

5:12-15 Proof of faith is shown in our way of life We work hard,
respect our leaders, live in peace and do not pay back wrongdoing but
show kindness to all v15.

5:16-18 Key to the Effective Victorious Life Joy, prayer and
thanksgiving, always – this is God's will for us. It is not that we must
give thanks for bad circumstances but that we give thanks to God in all
circumstances and in all things because of who he is – with a grateful
heart. This is our pattern of life - be filled with the Holy Spirit Eph
5:18-21 - rejoice in the Lord always Phil 4:4-9. We ignore this to our
own loss.

5:19-22 Thankfulness to God is the atmosphere in which the Holy
Spirit moves. When we live in continual thankfulness we do not put out
the Holy Spirit's fire but open our lives for him to work in and through us
v19; Acts 16:25-34. How often the Holy Spirit is grieved by our negative
thoughts, words and actions which do nothing to improve our situation
Eph 4:30.

5:23-28 Sanctification It is God who sanctifies us through the Holy
Spirit's leading – our whole spirit, soul and body.
We have confidence of all these things because they are based on God's
faithfulness – *the One who calls you is faithful and he will do it v23,24.*
This applies to all the promises in the Word of God.

Spirit, Soul and Body – the tripartite nature of the human being 1Thes 5:23

Most agree that the human being is unique in creation and that there is more than a physical body – the very concept of life and death indicate that something departs at death.

The materialist denies the spirit and sees the soul as the metaphysical part of the physical body Jude 1:19.

We must be guided by the revelation of Scripture.

The Bible reveals the human being as a unity - whole spirit, soul and body 1Thes 5:23.

Body God formed mankind from the dust of the earth – the physical body, flesh, the five senses (sight, sound, touch, taste, smell), made of the chemicals, the common elements of matter from the beginning Gen 2:7 – along with all other physical matter. The body returns to the dust Gen 3:19. These are now demonstrated facts.

We have a mind, a brain, controlling the functions of the body, explained by physics and biology.

Soul God breathed into man and he became a living soul Gen 2:7. The soul incorporates consciousness, thought, intellect, reason, integrity, emotions, desires, moral order – good and bad.

The soul is a real non-physical, immaterial part of us that interacts with the body. How this takes place is a mystery. Natural science cannot fathom how mindless order and objective matter has become subjective mind.

The soul is independent of the body – God is able to destroy both soul and body in hell Mt 10:28.

The soul of every living thing is in the hand of God and the breath of all mankind Job 12:10.

God takes away the soul of every person at death Job 27:8.

God holds the soul accountable - *behold, all souls are mine - the soul that sins, it shall die Ezk 18:4,20.*

The soul is where the moral decisions are made – the flesh, the body, wars against the soul Pet 2:11. There is also a degree of free will Jn 3:17,18.

Psychology, philosophy and beliefs are intangible concepts of the mind unless there is an outside source.

Jesus confirmed the presence of the soul – *do not be afraid of those who kill the body but cannot kill the soul. Rather be afraid of the One who* *can destroy both soul and body in hell Mt 10:28;* 16:26. He encourages us to love the Lord with all our heart and soul and mind and strength Mk 12:30.

The Tree of Knowledge symbolizes innocent and moral choice – eat and die, be separate from God Gen 2:17. The Tree of Life symbolizes eternal life - obey and live, forever Gen 3:22.

At the Fall mankind became separated from God - has become like one of us (no longer innocent) – they must not live forever (in an unregenerate state) Gen 3:22.

The soul of the unbeliever will be required to give account – the soul of the unrepentant will be held in hell till judgment Mt 12:36; Lk 12:19,20; Ps16:10.

Spirit Beyond the personal being is the awareness of God, the ability to relate to God - outside the realm of natural science which is restricted to physical pursuits.

God is revealed as Spirit Jn 4:24 – eternal (without beginning or end) and absolute (complete in all respects).

We are made in God's image, in God's likeness – not physical but soul and spirit Gen 1:26,27.

There is a natural body and a spiritual body 1Cor 15:44. The conflict between physical and spiritual is explained 1Cor 2:9-16.

The natural person, the body and soul, is limited to 'human thoughts' and struggles with God because the spirit is unresponsive. The person without the Spirit of God does not accept the 'things that come from the Spirit of God', for they are foolishness and cannot be understood because they are spiritually discerned 1Cor 2:14. The natural person cannot be subject to God Rom 8:5-8. The natural person is 'dead to God' Eph 2:1-3.

The human spirit must be regenerated in order to understand and embrace the things of God - to be 'born again' – to be 'made alive to God' Eph 2:4-10.

The spiritual person has the Spirit of God – they have the mind of Christ 1Cor 2:9-16; 1Jn 5:12.

Jesus explained - you must be born again – *to those who received him, who believed in his name he gave the right to become children of God – children born not of a natural descent or a husband's will, but born of God Jn 1:12,13. Flesh gives birth to flesh, but the Spirit gives birth to spirit Jn 3:3-8.*

When a person accepts Jesus Christ as Savior and Lord the spirit within is regenerated – born again by the operation of the Holy Spirit who then dwells within Eph 1:13,14.

This is the personal experience of those who take him at his word! The Spirit bears witness with our spirit that we are God's children Rom 8:16. The Spirit searches all things – the deep things of God. The Word of God divides soul and spirit Heb 4:12.

God is the Father of our spirits Heb 12:9 - the God of the spirits of all mankind Nu 16:22; 27:16

The first man Adam was made a living soul – the last Adam was made a quickening spirit 1Cor 15:45.

David acknowledged the soul - My soul thirsts for God, for the living God Ps 42:2

He addressed his soul - *Why are you cast down, O my soul? Ps 42:5.* There was another aspect of his being that desired to give praise to God apart from the soul and body. His whole being responded in praise - *Bless the LORD, O my soul, and forget not all his benefits Ps 103:2.* This also is the experience of the born again believer.

David knew the presence of the Holy Spirit and feared that the Spirit might be taken from him. Moses also knew this relationship Ex 33:14,15. Saul lost the presence of the Holy Spirit because he was not responsive. Mary also recognized her soul and her spirit Lk 1:46,47.

The Gospel This understanding of the nature of mankind and the consequence for each individual is the motivation for us to proclaim the good news of Jesus Christ to all people 2Tim 1:9,10.

2 Thessalonians

Introduction - A second letter of instruction was sent by Paul shortly after the first. Silas and Timothy were still with Paul.

Author - The apostle Paul writing from Corinth around AD 51.

Theme – The day of the Lord's return - further teaching on the end time.

THE SECOND COMING OF JESUS - (appearing - *parousia*)

1:1,2 **The Triune God** The believers have their foundation in relationship with God our Father and the Lord Jesus Christ 2:16.

1:3-5 **Growing in the face of Persecution** The new believers continued to grow in faith and love with perseverance despite persecutions and trials v4.

1:5 **Moral Order** All people have a sense of right and wrong. We feel sorrow when we see people suffer and a sense of guilt when we do what we perceive to be wrong. We perceive offense and demand justice especially for one's self. This universal recognition of moral order demands that justice be met.

Unjust persecution, deception and avoidance of responsibility all prove that God's judgment must come on evil v5.

1:6-10 **The Return of Jesus** God is just - his moral order will be vindicated when human history has run its course and his purpose has been served - justice and judgment will come. *This will happen when the Lord Jesus is revealed from heaven in blazing fire with his powerful angels – on the day he comes to be glorified in his holy people v7,10.*

Two Ways Jesus explained that he will return to earth again Mt 24:30. There will be two events which decide the future of each individual -

• **The elect** – He will gather the elect to be with him forever 1Thes 4:13-18 – the elect are those who have accepted him as Savior and Lord v8.

• **The unbeliever** - He will end rebellion and assemble the nations on earth to receive the consequences of their deeds Mt 25:31-33. It will result in punishment of those who have chosen to reject God and ignore his presence. The greatest loss for them will be separation from the presence of God for eternity v9.

Unbelievers do not expect the return of Jesus – they will be caught by surprise Mt 24:36-41. Believers live in expectation of this glorious and imminent event Mt 24:42; Rev 19:11-16.

1:11,12 **Jesus Will be Glorified** Paul prayed that God will provide power for every good purpose and act of faith in the believer so *the name of our Lord Jesus may be glorified in you and you in him! v11.* Believers will share in the final triumph over evil and in the future glory v10; Col 3:4; 1Jn 3:2.

The Culmination of Evil - the man of lawlessness

2:1-12 **The return of Jesus is assured** - but not *until the rebellion occurs and the man of lawlessness is revealed v3.* Paul had already taught about this v5.

From the beginning evil has been present Gen 3:1. There has been a continuing deterioration of the world order and many false teachings causing people to doubt the presence of God and his moral order v1,2. In the end time there will be an increase of evil (already at work v7) which will culminate in the revealing of a personification of evil. The evil will be contrary to the moral code of the Bible and in rebellion against God – the ultimate sin. As Satan sought to be equal with God so will his representative Is 14:12-14. The lawless one *will oppose and exalt himself over everything that is called God or is worshiped v4.* He will set himself up in the sanctuary (place of authority).

He will show miracles, signs and wonders as a counterfeit of Christ and will deceive many who will follow him – *who have not believed the truth but have delighted in wickedness v12.*

The antichrist This 'man of lawlessness' v3 was confirmed by John as the final antichrist - *who is coming - many have come - the man who denies that Jesus is the Christ, such a man is the antichrist - he denies the Father and the Son 1Jn 2:18-23.*

This figure compares with the 'little horn' of Daniel Dan 7:8 and two beasts identified in Revelation representing united world government and world ideology (religion) both under the ultimate control of the dragon, Satan Rev 12:3; 13:1,11.

Despite the apparent success of evil God is always in control – the extent of evil must be exhausted before all mankind will recognize God's rule. Examples of the lawless man are already at work, through the generations and in the present day. But evil is being held back till the proper time according to God's sovereign plan v6.

The King of kings and Lord of lords When the ultimate antichrist is revealed this lawless one will be overcome by the return of the Lord Jesus

- overthrown by the breath of his mouth and destroyed by the splendor of his coming v8; Rev 19:11-16.

2:13,14 Chosen by God Those who have received Jesus as Savior and Lord know that *from the beginning God chose you to be saved through the sanctifying work of the Spirit and through belief in the truth v13.* Because we responded to the Gospel we will *share in the glory of our Lord Jesus Christ v14.*

2:15-17 Confidence of our future The source of our *eternal encouragement and good hope is our Lord Jesus Christ and God our Father* (the Triune God) who will also encourage our hearts and strengthen us in everything we do *v16.*

3:1-5 Importance of Prayer Paul indicated his diligence in praying for the people 1:3,11. He asked them to pray for himself – for the rapid spread of the Gospel and deliverance from persecution. Prayer is essential, especially for those in the field.

3:6-15 Working for the Lord Work is not only necessary it is good for the body and soul. It was ordained by God at the Fall and included in the Fourth Commandment Gen 3:17-19; Ex 20:9. Jesus works with God the Father in the creation and he did the work of the Father in achieving our salvation Jn 5:17; 9:4.

The 'Protestant Work Ethic' has been one reason for the advance of the Western World and many personal successes.

Paul emphasized the importance of hard work and perseverance both personally and for the kingdom v6. However he lifted the motivation for all work to a new level when he requested that *whatever you do work at it with all your heart, as working for the Lord Col 3:23;* 1Cor 10:31; Eph 6:7. When we come to see ourselves in everything we do as **working for the Lord** we will make the best contribution and gain the greatest satisfaction from our labor and relationships.

3:16-18 The Lord of Peace The peace of Jesus, which passes all understanding and removes anxiety, which the world cannot give and cannot take away, is available at all times and in all circumstances to those who embrace him Mt 6:25-34; Jn 14:27; Phil 4:7.

1 Timothy

Introduction - Two pastoral letters were written to Paul's fellow worker Timothy who was given oversight of the believers in Ephesus. Timothy was a disciple at Lystra Acts 16:1 and traveled with Paul on his second and third mission journeys. He went to Corinth 1Cor 4:17 and Macedonia Acts 19:22 on behalf of Paul and stayed in Ephesus to oversee the believers when Paul had to leave quickly due to a riot Acts 20:1.

Author – Paul, possibly from Macedonia around AD 63.

Period – Possibly after Paul's release from detention in Rome.

Theme – Guidelines in leadership Instructions are given for appointing leaders and in administering the church. They are applicable in all leadership roles today and also in shaping our own lives.

Paul declared the authority for his ministry

1:1 **Apostle** – one sent on behalf of an authority to establish a significant work and to testify about Jesus.

1:2 By the command of God our Savior and of Christ Jesus our hope v1 The deity of Jesus and his equality within the Godhead is emphasized, both in nature and in salvation Phil 2:6.

1:3-7 **False Teaching** Timothy was placed at Ephesus in Paul's place to establish the new believers and to promote correct teaching. Controversy is a sign of errors in doctrine and does not promote God's work, faith in Christ or growth in the believer. It has assailed the believer since the first century. We need to be focused on the core issue of proclaiming the message of Jesus to the lost people of the world. Love must be the motivation for our efforts, not division v5.

1:8-11 **The purpose of the Law** Laws are for lawbreakers, not changed people. The Gospel sets us free from the regulations.

1:12-14 **The Grace of our Lord** When we come to faith in Jesus we recognize the offense of sin and are liberated from its power to live for him with new hearts and the indwelling presence of the Holy Spirit. Paul is an example of a changed person – once under the law - now saved by God's grace alone.

1:15-20 Christ Jesus came into the world to save sinners! v15 Paul came to see himself as the worst of sinners having persecuted the church and condoned the death of Stephen 1Cor 15:9; Gal 1:13. It is by recognition of our frailty and failures that the need for the Savior comes. We all need to seek and receive God's mercy through faith in Christ.

We can then live to bring honor and glory to *the King, eternal, immortal, invisible, the only God! v17.*

2:1-4 **Prayer and Thanksgiving** is a vital part of the ministry of each believer – for kings and leaders and then others - all whom God lays on our heart. God wants all people to be saved. Prayer is a vital part of this ministry v3.

2:5-7 **The Mediator** *There is one God and one mediator between God and men, the man Christ Jesus v5.* Jesus died to set us free from the penalty of sin - this is the core of the believer's message.

Leadership in the church

2:8-15 **Instructions for Leaders** Modesty and humility are important for women and men. Leadership should be recognized in either gender.

3:1-15 **Position Description** A task description with activities and responsibilities required for each position in the body with a character assessment listing qualities and skills should be documented. Examples for overseers (bishops) and deacons are given which are applicable for all leaders Acts 6:1-8.

3:16 **Jesus is our Example - God became Man in Jesus** - incarnate, raised from death, believed on and ascended in glory – this is a great mystery. Jesus must be our example as leaders and disciples in all things v16; Phil 2:5-11.

4:1-16 **Developing Godly Character and Conduct** Teaching should avoid restricting rules. The Gospel is about grace through faith in Jesus. Our aim is to strive to develop godly character and conduct through changed lives. Godly lives should first appear in the leaders v7. We place much emphasis on health and physical fitness which is important in this life. How much more important is it to focus on godliness and spiritual development which benefit as well in the life to come v8.

The critical role for a leader is to encourage others in the reading of the Word of God and in preaching and teaching v13.

A lifestyle that reflects the Lord Jesus Christ is the best way to bring others to the Lord v15. People will be influenced by our example. We should aim to be like him Rom 13:14.

Guidelines for all believers

5:1-25 **Attitude** We must develop the right attitude towards others and be responsible for our own actions. Respect all people. Provide for those in need. Give leaders their due recognition. Avoid favoritism and pursue good deeds v17. Let our attitude and deeds be our commendation. Jesus advised – *by their fruit you will know them Mt 7:15-20.*

6:1-10 Godliness with contentment is great gain Whatever our status or position we should respect those who are in authority. Avoid controversies, disputes and unwholesome talk.

Godliness with contentment, in life and service is a quality that is hard to achieve but brings great gain v6; Phil 4:12. We must recognize that all we are and have is given to us by God at his discretion. He has also provided all things for our glorious future. To understand this is the beginning of contentment.

If money or possessions become our goal we are open to many dangers and temptations v9,10. *No one serve two masters – you cannot serve both God and Money Mt 6:24.*

Pursuit of godliness Paul's teaching refutes the claim that he disregarded the law. He saw that the believer was released from the law in order to live a godly life by following Christ.

6:11-21 Fight the good fight of faith *v12* If we are to achieve anything worthwhile it requires effort and commitment. Life is a struggle especially if we are really committed to Jesus because the devil will come against us to try to make us give up and become ineffective v12; Eph 6:12; 1Pet 5:8. We must avoid evil, pursue good and live eternal life (actually we have entered into eternal life already – we will never die Jn 11:25,26). We have been given everything we have v13. We may enjoy all of God's provisions, but be generous and willing to share. In this way we are laying up treasure for the coming age!

Those who live only for this life miss out on the life to come. Those who apply God's principles of holiness and service take hold of the life that is eternal v19.

6:15,16 God, the blessed and only Ruler, the King of kings and the Lord of lords, who alone is immortal and who lives in unapproachable light, whom no one has seen or can see – this is our God, yet he chooses to seek us and we will dwell with him in eternity! Is 57:15,16; Rev 21:3.

2 Timothy

Introduction – This second pastoral letter from Paul to Timothy in Ephesus was written while Paul was in prison in Rome either for the first time in AD 60 or a second time in AD 65.

Author – The apostle Paul.

Period – Some years after the first letter.

Theme – **Making Disciples** An encouragement to remain faithful and bold under opposition. It was the command of Jesus that all believers should become disciples Mt 28:19.

Guidelines are given for strengthening the church for effective ministry so Timothy could be free to visit Paul in Rome.

THE CALL TO DISCIPLESHIP

1:1-6 **Prayer ministry** is vital for a disciple and for a disciple maker – night and day! We also must *fan into flame the gift of God* through the spiritual disciplines of prayer, reading the Word, worship, fellowship and witnessing.

1:7 **God has given us a spirit of power, of love and of self-discipline** – not of fear or timidity. Self-discipline is an aspect of the fruit of the Spirit and means bringing 'self' under the control of the Holy Spirit Gal 5:23.

1:8-13 **Bold testimony about Jesus** We are saved and called to be holy because of God's own purpose and grace - *this grace was given us in Christ Jesus before the beginning of time! v9.* **Jesus has destroyed death** This is the great assurance we have that no one else can provide. We now have life and immortality through the Gospel v10. We will not be ashamed if we know Jesus – who we have believed and are convinced that he is able to guard what we have entrusted to him for that day! v12. We endure suffering by the power of God.

1:13-18 **Making Disciples** Paul taught those he led to the Lord and developed them to become disciples, committed followers of Christ, so that they could, in turn disciple others.

The Basis for Small Group Ministry

2:1,2 **Discipling Strategy** Paul would gather believers (Timothy, Titus, Silas) into a small group and disciple them v2. He would develop them in the spiritual disciplines sharing his relationship with Jesus with them. He would then send them out as leaders to enlist others in small groups to disciple them. Paul learned this technique from Jesus and the example of the disciples. Jesus called individuals to himself, trained them and sent them out to apply and practice their skills Mt 10:1; Lk 10:1. He actually spent three years making twelve disciples - pouring himself into them!

Delegation and multiplication This was also the instruction of Jethro to Moses – the principle of delegation Ex 18:13-26. It is the most effective way to make strong disciples and the key to effectively reproducing ministry. Nehemiah also demonstrated the value of small groups Neh 3:1-32.

The small group leader will share their relationship with Jesus together with the group members – they apply the spiritual disciplines with them Ecc 4:9. They seek to lead others into the presence of Jesus -

• **Christ Centered** - the aim is to make Christ preeminent and be in his presence together
• **Christ Like** – they seek to become Christ like
• **Christ Doing** – they find ways to do what Jesus did.

They learn to appropriate the promise of Jesus Mt 18:20.
In small groups do not neglect the spiritual dimension!

Disciples make disciples To become a disciple, like an apprentice or learner-driver requires more than theory – it is necessary to be exposed to application and practice in the presence of and under the guidance of a skilled person - this is how multiplication works. You cannot make disciples if you are not one yourself – you cannot lead an effective small group without your own relationship with Jesus.

2:3-13 **The life of a disciple** is like a soldier who will endure hardship because he wants to please his commanding officer - our Commander is Jesus. In the same way a competing athlete has to do the work and complete the course to win the prize and a hardworking farmer may expect to share the harvest v5,6. The result of our efforts will bring salvation with eternal glory - for us and for those we serve v8-10.

We have a great promise – if we died to the world with Jesus we will live eternally with him - if we endure with him we will reign with him v11-13.

2:14-19 **A Skilled Workman** A born again believer becomes a worker for the kingdom - a disciple. We must each do our best – give all our effort to be *a workman - who correctly handles the word of truth* - the Word of God *v15*. This demands diligence in reading, studying, memorizing and meditating on God's Word. We need to become approved to God each day so we will not have to be ashamed in any respect. Handling the Word means to be able to help others understand it and to know how to direct them to the important verses to address their needs and to grow. We must know how to lead others to Christ using verses in the Word Rom 3:21-31. We should learn to correct errors and guide people in the truth using the Word. We must first be appropriating and applying the Word in our own lives.

2:20-26 **An Instrument for Noble Use** In this way each one of us has the opportunity *to cleanse oneself to be an instrument for noble purposes, made holy, useful to the Master and prepared to do any good work v20,21.* It requires pursuing righteousness, faith, love and peace and calling on the Lord out of a pure heart. As we do this we become more available for effective use by the Lord. Always remember we are pots of clay, yet we contain great treasure - so that the all-surpassing power of our work is of God and not of us 2Cor 4:7.

Leadership must be gentle with others hoping to bring them to the truth.

Warning about Persecution in the Last Days

3:1-14 **The last days will be known by terrible times** – people will follow self-centeredness with a form of goodness but denying God. Those who follow God will face persecution v12.

THE POWER and PURPOSE OF THE WORD OF GOD

3:16,17 **The power and focus** of the believer's life is the Word of God -
• the Bible contains all you need to know in order to be saved – it is able to make you wise for salvation v15
• the Bible is God-breathed – the Holy Spirit inspired the authors by breathing into them, so that they recorded what God wanted them to write - both Old and New Testament – it is God's Word to us today 2Pet 1:20,21
• The Holy Spirit will breath into you whenever you open and read it in his presence - he will speak to you, encourage you and direct you as you listen to him v16
• *it is necessary for teaching, rebuking, correcting and training in righteousness* - we must expect to experience these spiritual insights and directions as we read it and regularly take time to hear 2Thes 2:13
• the reason for this is *so that the person of God may be thoroughly equipped for very good work v17.* God will use us effectively as we equip

ourselves with his Word, by reading it regularly, understanding it and committing it to memory.

The Word of God The 'Word' included the Old Testament Scriptures and the teaching of Jesus and his whole way of life Mt 4:4; Lk 24:44-46; Jn 1:1,14. The writings of the New testament are now included embracing in total some 40 authors over 1,500 years Rom 15:4; 1Cor 2:13; 10:11.

4:1-8 **Always be ready and prepared to share your faith with others** – everything you have learned about God - on every occasion v2. We don't know what impact our words will have on the hearers. Be prepared means -

• know in a few short words how to tell someone how you came to believe in Jesus and what he means to you
• know where to find verses to confirm what you believe
• know how to lead someone to Jesus from the Bible - the Plan of Salvation Rom 3:21-31 (ref p7).

Many will turn to false teaching. Our task is to proclaim the true message under all circumstances and to persevere.

If we fight the good fight, finish the race and keep the faith, we will receive the crown of righteousness – we will live with Jesus forever v6-8.

Personal Matters

4:9-22 Paul wanted Timothy's fellowship. Luke was still with him and he wanted Mark to come to Rome v11. Strong fellowship with other believers is vital to spiritual growth Pro 27:17.

We may be assured that God will rescue us in every trial and bring us safely to his heavenly kingdom v18.

Priscilla had become a home group leader v19.

Reasons for a Daily Devotion

A consistent devotional life is the way to walk with the Lord and to be effective in serving him. Spend special time each day with God – read his Word, pray, meditate, listen. Apply the truths, values, principles and promises of God's Word in your daily life Eph 1:3.

1. Fellowship – communicate with God. This is the reason you were created and redeemed Heb 10:19-22
- take time to thank and praise him Ps 100:4
- learn to walk in the Spirit – listen and respond Jn 4:23,24.

2. Dedication - each day renew your trust Rom 12:1,2
- check your program with the Lord 1 Sam 23:2,4,10.

3. Our Need - we need time with the Lord Is 40:31
- acknowledge your need – thirst Ps 63:1,2
- He is your source of power Eph 1:17-20
- *Blessed are those who hunger and thirst for righteousness for they will be filled Mt 5:6.*

4. Guidance - His Word keeps us on track 2Tim 3:16
- ask him to search your heart Ps 139:23-24
- He will make your path straight Pro 3:5,6
- He will lead you in the things he wants you to do Ps 32:8.

5. Staying on Course
- always come back to the Lord after a storm Ps 51.

6. The Example of Others – Mk 1:35; Lk 6:12; Mt 14:23
- you need a time, a place, a habit Dan 6:10
- you need a method – a plan, to keep you focused and balanced on the whole Word.

7. Become proficient in the Word
- the devil knows the power of the Word and is afraid
- the Bible will make you come alive
- memorize the Word and meditate on it Jos 1:8; Ps 119:11
- the Holy Spirit uses the Word – he calls it to remembrance, when we absorb it Jn 14:26.

Titus

Introduction – Titus was a fellow worker with Paul. He accompanied him on his visit to Jerusalem after the first mission journey and on other journeys Gal 2:1. He was given oversight of the church in Crete.

Author – Paul, possibly from Macedonia around AD 63.

Period – Possibly after Paul's release from prison in Rome.

Theme – Role of Leaders This pastoral letter gives guidelines in appointing leaders and in administering the church.

Qualities for Leaders and Believers

1:1-4 **Gospel summary** Faith in Christ leads to godliness – results in eternal life – promised by God before the beginning of time – brought to light at the right time – by the preaching of the Gospel of Jesus Christ.

1:4-9 **Leaders** – elders and overseers (bishops) must show good conduct in their private lives. They must teach the people with sound doctrine and encouragement.

1:10-16 **Refuting false teaching** Leaders must denounce deceptive and wrong teaching, especially the pressure to adopt Jewish customs. Many were being led astray by these people.

2:1-15 **Guidelines for specific groups** The godly conduct of the Christian Way embraces all areas of life and relations with other people, ages, gender and classes – in many cases they are opposite to the natural way of the world. We are required to deny ungodliness and worldly passions with self-control and integrity.

The return of Jesus We wait in expectation of the coming of Jesus who died to redeem us from our sins and purify us to himself.

3:1-8 **The reason for our way of life** God saved us by rebirth and the Holy Spirit through Jesus – *having been justified by his grace we become heirs having the hope of eternal life v7.*

3:9-15 **Warnings** Avoid controversy, arguments and quarrels that achieve nothing but division and discouragement.

3:12-15 **Further plans** Paul wanted to meet Titus in Nicopolis on the west coast of Greece and spend the winter there. He was already arranging a replacement for Crete ever planning for the welfare of the believers.

Philemon

Introduction - Philemon was a leader in the church at Colossae and a friend of Paul. Onesimus was a slave who stole money from Philemon and fled to Rome where he was brought to faith in Jesus by Paul.
Author – The apostle Paul around AD 60.
Period – A teaching letter while Paul was in prison in Rome.
Theme – Forgiveness A request to forgive someone who had done wrong.

1:1-3 The early church met mostly in the homes of believers.

1:4-7 **A model prayer for other believers** Thankfulness for them that they might be active in witnessing and that they might have a full understanding of every good thing we have in Christ.

1:8-21 **The Power of Forgiveness** Paul requested Philemon to forgive Onesimus and restore him to his previous duty.

Paul knew the power of forgiveness. He had been forgiven for the death of Stephen and his strenuous persecution of the believers. He had been restored – the burden removed.

There is every reason for forgiveness –
- It is the character of God to forgive 1Jn 1:9
- Jesus demonstrated the supreme act of forgiveness Lk 23:34
- We have been forgiven that great debt of ours Mt 18:32
- Unwillingness to forgive produces bitterness and primarily hurts oneself – it is a burden that is no benefit to us and which we do not have to bear
- Unresolved issues create enmity on our part with the other party which is unhelpful and unnecessary
- God will forgive us as we forgive others – he wants to see his nature formed in us Mt 6:14,15
- We are encouraged to forgive our enemies Mt 5:43-48

The request was made to forgive Onesimus on the strength of Paul's relationship with Philemon – this is real friendship.

23-25 Mark and Luke were together as Paul's fellow workers. It was around this time that they were each working on their Gospel accounts!

Prayer – The Power, the Privilege and the Purpose

1. Approach - the purpose of prayer is spiritual communication
Jesus taught us how to pray – he gave us a model Matt 6:1–15; Lk 11:1-13 -
- Our Father – we are drawn into a relationship – personal, conversational Gal 4:6
- Who is in Heaven – we are drawn into a location Heb 10:19-22
- Holy is your Name – we are in a presence Is 6:1-7
- Your Kingdom come – we focus on the purpose of creation – we give our commitment Rev 11:15
- Your will be done on earth as it is in heaven – our submission and effort Mt 7:21; Jn 5:30
- Give us today – freedom from anxiety Mt 6:25-34
  - Our daily bread – a statement of trust, each day
- Forgive us our trespasses – freedom from burdens
  - As we forgive others – a condition Mt 6:14,15 - the unmerciful servant Mt 18:21-35
- Lead us, not into temptation – we will be tested and tempted Lk 22;40,46; 1Cor 10:13
- But deliver us from evil – seek leading and guidance 1Pet 5:8
- For yours is the kingdom, the power and the glory for ever – Amen.

The first five points of this model involve worship and commitment. Compare your prayer with the praise of Heaven Rev 4:8-11; 5:8-14; 7:9-17.

2. Attitude – we need to have the right condition of mind
- The Beatitudes set the conditions of the kingdom Mt 5:1-16
- The conduct and attitude of members of the kingdom Mt 5:1-48
- The lifestyle of members of the kingdom Eph 4:1-4
- Acceptance of the Father's will Lk 22:42;43 - God is changing us - he is more concerned with our character than our comfort
- We are working with the Holy Spirit – who helps us in our weakness Rom 8:26,27.

3. Application Our Father wants the best for us Mt 6:32; 7:9-11
- Have confidence in God 1Jn 5:14-15
- Have boldness in faith Jas 5:13-18
- Be persistent - ask and keep on asking Mt 7:7-12
  - The shameless neighbor – because of his boldness Lk 11:5-13
  - The persistent widow and the unjust judge – to show us that we should always pray and not give up Lk 18:1-8
- Be unwavering, single-minded – don't be disqualified by doubt Jas 1:8
- Pray in the name of Jesus Jn 14:16.

4. Authority We have the command and the authority of God 1Tim 2:14
- *By me kings reign – by me princes govern Prov 8:15-16*
- *He reduces the rulers of this world to nothing Is 40:23*
- *The Most High is sovereign over the kingdoms of men and gives them to anyone he wishes and sets over them the lowliest of men Dan 4:17*
- *There is no authority except that which God has established Rom 13:1*
- *Ask the Lord of the harvest to send out workers into his harvest field Mt 9:38*
- *The prayers of the saints went up before God Rev 8:4.*

Outline of the Epistles

Epistles of Paul

Epistle	date	from	theme
First Mission Journey			
Galatians	AD 49	Antioch	Freedom from the Law through faith in Christ Jesus.
Second Mission Journey			
1 Thessalonians	AD 51	Corinth	Holiness of living. Christ's return.
2 Thessalonians	AD 51	Corinth	The Day of the Lord's return.
Third Mission Journey			
1 Corinthians	AD 55	Ephesus	Instruction in daily living & spiritual gifts
2 Corinthians	AD 56	Macedonia	Guidelines in discipleship
Romans	AD 57	Corinth	God's gift of righteousness by faith in Christ alone
Prison Epistles			
Ephesians	AD 60	Rome	New life in Christ. Spiritual warfare
Philippians	AD 60	Rome	The joy of living for Christ.
Colossians	AD 60	Rome	The supremacy of Christ & the Gospel
Philemon	AD 60	Rome	Forgiveness.
Further Journeys & Prison			
1 Timothy	AD 63	Macedonia	Leadership Manual
Titus	AD 63	Macedonia	Conduct for Christian Living
2 Timothy	AD 66	Rome	Endurance in pastoral ministry

General Epistles

Epistle	date	from	theme
Hebrews	AD 65	unknown	The Gospel of Jesus Christ is superior to the Old Covenant in all respects
James	AD 48	Jerusalem	Genuine faith produces action
1 Peter	AD 65	Rome	The glory of the believer's inheritance
2 Peter	AD 65	Rome	Warning against false teaching.
1 John	AD 90	Patmos	Deity of Jesus & assurance of salvation
2 John	AD 90	Patmos	Continue in love as we follow Jesus.
3 John	AD 90	Patmos	Be faithful in leadership.
Jude	unknown	Jerusalem	Beware of false teachers.
Revelation	AD 90	Patmos	Sovereignty of God & return of Jesus

BOOKS OF THE BIBLE

[39 + 27 = 66]

BOOKS OF THE OLD TESTAMENT

		[39]		
	HISTORY (17)	**POETRY (5)**	**PROPHECY (17)**	
LAW (5)	Genisis	Job	Isaiah	**MAJOR (5)**
Pentateuch	Exodus	Psalms	Jeremiah	
Books of Moses	Leviticus	Proverbs	Lamentations	
	Numbers	Ecclesiastes	Ezekiel	
	Deuteronomy	Solomon	Daniel	
HISTORY (12)	Joshua		Hosea	**MINOR (12)**
of Israel	Judges		Joel	
	Ruth		Amos	
	1 Samuel		Obadiah	
	2 Samuel		Jonah	
	1 Kings		Micah	
	2 Kings		Nahum	
	1 Chronicles		Habakkuk	
	2 Chronicles		Zephaniah	
	Ezra	Post Exile	Haggai	
	Nemiah		Zechariah	
	Esther		Malachi	

BOOKS OF THE NEW TESTAMENT

		[27]		
	HISTORY (5)	**LETTERS OF PAUL (13)**	**GENERAL LETTERS (9)**	
GOSPELS (4)	Matthew	Romans	Hebrews	Unknown
	Mark	1 Corinthians	James	Other
	Luke	2 Corinthians	1 Peter	Apostles (7)
	John	Glatians	2 Peter	
Early Church (1)	Acts	Ephesians	1 John	
Luke		Philippians	2 John	
		Colossians	3 John	
		1 Thessalonians	Jude	
		2 Thessalonians	Revelation	John
		1 Timothy		
		2 Timothy		
		Titus		
		Philemon